Common Approach

UnCommon Results

How adoption delivers the results you deserve

D0652621

Common
Approach
UnCommon
Results

How adoption delivers
the results you deserve

Ian Gotts

**Includes a 5-step blueprint for action
by Richard Parker**

www.Ideas-Warehouse.com

Published by Ideas-Warehouse

Old Theatre

Stansted Park

Rowlands Castle

Hampshire

PO9 6DX

www.Ideas-Warehouse.com

ISBN 978-0-9548309-1-5

Text and images © Ideas-Warehouse 2004
Second edition © Ideas-Warehouse 2007

Written by Ian Gotts and Richard Parker

*All rights reserved. Apart from the purposes of review, criticism,
research or private study, no part of this publication may be
reproduced, stored in a retrieval system or transmitted, in any form or
by any means, electronic, mechanical, recording or otherwise, in any
part of the world, without the prior permission of the publisher.
Requests for permission should be sent to the publisher at the address
given above.*

Design and layout by Studio 183, Thorney

Cover design by GTM Ltd

Printed and bound in Italy by LegoPrint SpA

Contents

Acknowledgements

To our clients who have proven that this is not theory, but delivers tangible results.[1]

[1]And have paid us as well.

Foreword

Managing business change is challenging. You only have to look at the statistics of success and failure to recognise that reality. The desired outcomes or objectives may be well defined, but getting there is much less certain, and there are many obstacles to be overcome along the way. However, managing change is not some esoteric art form or random process. There are some proven ways of understanding change as well as proven tools and techniques to help enable and manage it.

Critically, change is about changing behaviours, and achieving new levels of performance as a result, whether the change be caused by new systems, or new organisation, or new process. This book explores the key issues of behavioural change and the idea of adoption or the rate of adoption as the ultimate test of successful change. Ian's $R=IA^2$ formula neatly captures the essence of the relationship between results and how well the intended change is adopted.

The Accenture Institute for High Performance interviewed executives from 14 industries to identify the major reasons why change initiatives fail to get results. 64% said the greatest reason was 'Lack of buy-in that change is necessary'. Further, all the issues identified centred on commitment to change – in other words on the issue of adoption.

This book first helps managers at all levels to understand the real change management and adoption challenge. And recognising that challenge is half the battle. But the book then suggests practical and achievable approaches to getting consistent adoption both across and up and down the organisation. It is based on real client experience Ian has gained over many years both with Accenture and with Nimbus where he has developed some tools and techniques that can make a real difference in helping to enable successful change.

Someone once defined insanity as doing the same thing over and over and expecting different results. The blueprint for action – the 5-Step approach described in this book – helps anyone engaged in a transformation initiative validate that they are on the right track, and if necessary make course corrections so that they will get the results that they expect.

Having worked with Ian over a number of years, I am delighted that he has found time to write a book which is a positive addition to the thinking and writing on this topic, and can help develop people's understanding of managing change.

Peter Cheese

Global Managing Partner –
Human Performance Service Line, Accenture

Accenture is a global management consulting, technology services and outsourcing company.

Who should read this book

'Either lead, follow, or get out of my way.' Credo of Ted Turner

This book contains many of the things we have seen work at many successful companies, some of whom have become our clients over the years. It's a practical guide, which means that we've tried to make it clear and action-oriented.

You might ask who we have written this book for. The answer is you...

- If you are in charge of strategy development, here's a book that will help drive your strategy (and its updates) through your organisation.

- If you are in process management working to make your company more agile and perform better, we feel your pain.

- If you are charged with automating processes to improve efficiency and compliance.

- If you are in compliance, you're King these days. Stay that way by helping your company to work flexibly and focus on the results rather than simply providing compliance.

- If you are leading a major software implementation there are approaches that will help you be among the 30% of projects that actually gets a ROI.

- If you intend to occupy your role until retirement, wake up and get involved.

Why we wrote this book

Over the last ten years we have worked with many clients and developed a proven platform for change and business management that supports the deployment and ongoing measurement.

The framework and approach we have developed supports and leverages a variety of standard business methodologies and drives improved ROI across a range of initiatives that you are either already conducting or about to embark on.

We learned a lot about why developing an intelligent operations manual works to execute change and make it stick. Rapid results and step changes are possible and often a reality, but to really have a lasting impact on your business, this approach needs to be driven from the leadership teams of organisations over a sustained period.

Our clients have helped us grow these principles to proven success. Enterprises large and small have proven these techniques in this book on a global scale, while others with smaller tactical projects are microcosms of a quiet revolution.

If you apply the knowledge in this book, you will have the platform to run your business more effectively, drive more ROI from existing and future change initiatives and understand how and where to act to get ever better at turning your Strategy into Reality.

Using this book

This book is intended to be the catalyst for action. We hope that the ideas and examples inspire you to act. So, do whatever you need to make this book useful. Use Post-it notes, photocopy pages, scan pages. Go to our website and email colleagues the e-book summary. Lend it. Rip it apart, or read it quickly in one go. Whatever works for you.[3]

 You will notice that we have highlighted ideas, thoughts and actions throughout this book. If they don't spur you to act, you should at least find them thought-provoking and they may inspire ideas of your own...

We hope this becomes your most dog-eared book.

Send us your feedback

We love feedback. We prefer great reviews, but we'll accept anything which helps us take the ideas further. The ideas have been the result of every single person we have worked with in our careers in performance management. We welcome your comments on this book.

We'd prefer email as it's easy to answer and saves trees. If the ideas worked for you we'd love to hear your success stories. That's why we're doing it.

Ian@Ideas-Warehouse.com
Richard@Ideas-Warehouse.com
Tel: +44 800 358 0037

The Old Theatre
Stansted Park
Rowlands Castle
Hampshire
PO9 6DX
United Kingdom

www.Ideas-Warehouse.com

Then get our next book which will be based on that feedback...

[3] If you copy the chapters, then be sure to look at at least one other book – then it is research and not plagiarism.

PART I: From strategy to reality

Chapter 1

From strategy to reality – R=IA²

'It's no secret what needs to be done. The challenge is to put the strategy, systems and capabilities in place and then drive deployment and execution.'

A.G. Lafley, CEO of Procter & Gamble

Everyone needs a strategy...

Where is your strategy? Hidden in the annual report? In the minds of the Executive Team? Or is it where it should be – spelt out in the values, KPIs, processes and organisation of the operation.

I'm not talking about pithy vision or mission statements. What I'm looking for is something that every member of staff uses to make their day-to-day decisions. Here is not the place to discuss formulation of strategy. This is about execution of strategy.

... but it's execution that counts

A real business leader sets vision and direction, creates the framework (people, processes, measures) and prioritises activities (based on allocation of budget). And then paints a picture of the successful outcome. A clear, simple story that inspires and motivates.

What separates the exceptional performers from the average is NOT the quality of their strategies. It's their ability to execute them. General George Patton had it right when he said:

'A good plan violently executed right now is far better than a perfect plan executed next week.'

The Hay Group, in its research from 346 companies into what

makes a Most Admired Company for *Fortune* magazine, interviewed 10,000 Directors from two groups of companies in the same industry sector – the Most Admired and their peers.

When asked to respond to the statement: 'We have translated our strategy into clear action plans with clear accountabilities', 84% of respondents in the Most Admired Companies agreed, against 74% for the peer group.

This was consistent from industry sector to industry sector, so there is nowhere to hide, as I can hear you saying 'Ah, but our industry is not like those surveyed. We're different.' Clearly, management at these companies know how to get their point across and their strategies executed. And there is something we can learn from them.

 Walk around your organisation and ask people what they think the company does.

Why is implementing a strategy such a difficult thing to do?

People implement strategies... successfully or otherwise, which is why the smart money is on companies – such as our Most Admired Companies – that work to develop their people. Procter & Gamble, for example, holds line managers responsible for talent reviews and dealing with poor performers. And because people execute your strategy, you need to include and engage each and every one of them.

 There is no substitute for a coherent plan entertainingly communicated to a dedicated workforce who are able and willing to execute at all levels of the company.

I've defined a formula that is fundamental to the way a strategy is translated into action. I've called it the 'Fundamental Law of Business':[1]

R=IA²
(Results = Initiatives x Adoption²)

[1] In line with the fundamental law of physics $E=mc^2$.

Maximising Results by successful Adoption of the changes driven out of the Initiatives

What this equation reveals is that it doesn't matter how many initiatives (projects, exercises, programmes, whatever) you throw at people if no one adopts their results. Typical initiatives include Six Sigma, SAP implementation, Cost Reduction, Customer First and CRM change programmes.

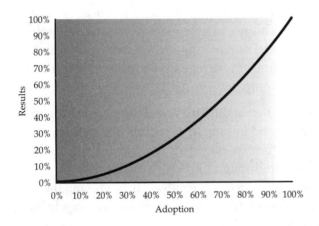

That adoption is significantly more important (hence adoption squared[2]) is shown by the graph, above. If adoption is measured as a percentage of the adoption of the organisation, then 50% adoption gets you 25% of the result. If 90% adoption, it is 81% of the result.

But here is the critical bit – if adoption is 0%, then the result is 0 and you get nowhere.

Most companies focus a lot (or all) of their efforts on 'I' (initiatives), while 'A' (adoption) never gets formalised. Perhaps adoption is too difficult to specify, and often it gets called training – and that is the first budget to be cut when the Initiative overruns. Additionally, adoption is often left until the Initiative has been completed and is fully in place, rather than woven into the overall Initiative from the beginning.

[2] At a recent Software Leaders' lunch, the CEO of a major financial services software company challenged me. After 25 years implementing software he said that it shouldn't be 'A' squared, but R=IAⁿ where 'n' was a large number.

Look at the way many companies are approaching Sarbanes-Oxley or Basel II compliance, thinking about initiatives rather than adoption. This is seen as the project being run by the Compliance Officer – an activity designed to get a 'tick in the box' that involves as few people as possible. But compliance is everybody's issue in building a business that works effectively.

Adoption means integrating the new way of working, driven by any initiatives or the strategy, in the context of everyone's job. This goes far beyond measurement, even though it does take its cue from the numbers, primarily because these numbers are (usually) already universally used throughout the company.

However, adoption is difficult to 'sell' to people because it seems so vague and imprecise. It sounds like training. The benefits need to be explained to them. Interestingly, once people have been through projects that have failed and recognise the root cause of the failure, they become the most ardent supporters of adoption. You can see the cogs turning when you write the formula up on the whiteboard – and then see comprehension explode in their eyes.[3]

The ultimate 'A-ha' effect.

The approach to adoption

You need an approach that focuses on getting your strategic improvement efforts *really* understood and used by everyone in the company.

You do that by bringing people together and ensuring that there is involvement – not in strategy formulation, but in the application of its key points throughout the company. By this I mean the changes in behaviour, the changed working practices, the new tools and techniques required by the whole company. The approach to adoption creates a shared language (which I explain in chapter 7) that everyone can understand, so everyone in turn understands their part and context in the strategy.

[3]Interestingly, people can relate to this at every level in the organisation.

'How can I apply the strategy in my day-to-day work?' is the recurrent theme to this approach. Key is the emphasis on processes, i.e. how do we get the job done successfully and who is accountable for each task? This focus directly helps people to leverage any strategic improvements within the context of their daily tasks.

You drive real adoption (and thus different behaviour) into your company by focusing on process. You have to spend time with your teams at each level in your business and define their end-to-end processes.

 The alternative to embedding processes in day-to-day behaviour is to either check people's work to death OR tell them what NOT to do, or a combination of both.

Why is this so important?

Because we're all responsible for delivering great value to our shareholders, employees and customers – against increasing competition, increasing regulation, and in a more and more complex world. We have a responsibility to get the best out of our companies, which means getting the best out of the people, including ourselves.

Every one of us needs to be proud of, feel part of, and understand how we contribute to the success of the business. That is high performance in business. That is converting strategy to reality.[4]

---

[4] If that is not the desire, then it is better not to have even had a strategy in the first place. That's what is called a hobby or an idle pastime.

Chapter 2

Results

'However beautiful the strategy, you should occasionally look at the results.'

Sir Winston Churchill

What are you aiming for?

So, what do you want your strategy to achieve? For some companies this is the vision or mission. But it is more than that. We've all seen mission statements like 'To be the leading provider of healthcare', but that just isn't precise enough.

What is the most important aspect of this vague mission statement, in terms of revenue, product leadership, profit or market share? Which are the key drivers, and in what order of priority and context?

Directives in the Chairman's statement in the annual report tell you what the company wants to achieve, but which is the most important?[1] Typically there are statements like these:

- Launch in three new regions next year…

- Cut costs by 15% in US…

- Increase revenue by 25%…

- Increase margin by 13% over the next three years…

- Outsource manufacturing to cut costs by 26%…

- Have 60% of revenue from products that are less than two years old.

You need to decide what the most important results your strategy needs to deliver are. It can be pretty difficult to

[1] These are objectives that people can aspire to, can work towards, can celebrate when they are achieved, and correct the course when they are missed. I am not motivated by an objective of a 6.4% Return on Capital Employed. Maybe the accountants or actuaries among you are.

select these key priorities for an organisation, but there are lots of strategy books out there to help, so we won't repeat this here. Instead, we are going to concentrate on how to implement the strategy, whatever it may be.

Setting objectives, getting results

Results aren't just the impressive figures you publish in your annual report. Think of your objectives:

- For the whole company
- For just a division
- For the function you are responsible for.

Here are a few sample results set as objectives, to inspire you:

Results from an SAP implementation:
'...although the software upgrade is forced upon us we will use this to re-engineer underperforming processes – better efficiencies, especially in back office staffing and procurement, will drive a 12% reduction in costs.'

Results from Outsourcing:
Provide the business with outside expertise and capital, to make the business as a whole more agile. We will be able to launch a new product in 4 months rather than 7 months.

Result from supply chain initiatives:
Get our production forecasting 10% more accurate so we eliminate discounting and rushing custom-build, saving $120m annually.

Result from a quality initiative:
We get through ISO 9000 every year, but in reality people don't do what's in the procedures – that's just to get the certificate – we estimate that this costs the business $70m annually plus the time spent preparing for the annual audits.

 Draw a small box just big enough for a number. When you measure the results, write it in the box. Note: the box isn't big enough for an excuse, story or reason.

Leadership – setting goals for the organisation

Effective leadership and sustainable organisational success are both on the same side of the coin. Employees and management expect leadership to create the direction, alignment and commitment that will enable them to achieve organisational success.

But creating direction, alignment and commitment – the work of leadership – is becoming more difficult than ever. Change is permanent. In a survey by Cap Gemini Ernst & Young, 86 executives identified the top three threats that they and their organisations will face in the next two years. The executives cited regulatory changes (38%), competitive dynamics (29%) and market uncertainty (19%). All these concerns are related to change.

Yet you cannot afford to walk around with a worried look on your face. As the CEO or CFO or Divisional Head, a lot of people are relying on you 'directing the ship' safely and effectively. Employees, customers and shareholders all look to you. You are leader, coach and cheerleader. You cannot afford to stumble. More importantly, you cannot do it by yourself. You need to develop and engender a 'performance management culture' and get the team on board.

 Ask some of your employees what measures influence their day-to-day decisions.

Delivering results

In every major corporation there is change: externally imposed change (customers, competition, regulation) and internally imposed change (growth and profitability targets). Few, if any, companies are in a position where they are in a steady state, or where they are continuously improving – the 'mythical learning organisation'. Most companies drive changes through a series of initiatives. The larger the organisation the more overlapping initiatives there are. It is the delivery of the changes from these initiatives that delivers the results. Initiatives are the 'engines of change'. So we need to look to the effective delivery of these initiatives to be able to deliver the results our business and our shareholders need.[2] Which is why the formula $R=IA^2$ strikes a chord with every top-level executive I talk to.

[2]Which is what the CEO and management's sole focus should be.

Chapter 3

Initiatives

'Everyone who has ever run anything in their lives spends more time stopping new things than starting new things. You have to ruthlessly stamp on new initiatives.'

Sir John Harvey-Jones, former chairman of ICI

Just a few initiatives

If your company is anything like many I have worked with over the years, you will have a number of initiatives in progress:

- A large consulting firm installing a new budgeting system in the UK. If successful, it will be installed in other countries over two years.

- A strategy firm working on a complexity cost project across your key product lines in your main production plant, in the US.

- Your purchasing department completing a multi-country procurement evaluation...

- ...and it is involved in a supply chain project together with your logistics department, piloted in Spain.

- Your Human Resources department is reviewing your recruitment process.

- The auditors are conducting a Sarbanes-Oxley compliance review across the group.

- and the list goes on.

Oh, and by the way, you are also still installing parts of your enterprise resource planning (ERP) system – an initiative that started two years ago. And now you are thinking about merging with a similar-sized company.

Lots of initiatives can spring up almost invisibly, launched within the budgets of the local sponsor, and with parallel initiatives in the next department. While many existing initiatives are all fighting for resources and management time, new initiatives quietly mushroom unnoticed by those looking at the bigger picture. Unchecked, lots of other initiatives spring up, all launched within the funding sign-off limits of the local sponsor – often without visibility of a similar initiative in the next silo[1] along the corridor. Sometimes it may look like any approach to co-ordinating these projects has gone out of the window.

The big issue in companies is having a holistic co-ordinating approach across the many initiatives which all demand management time, resources and funding.

 On a sheet of paper, write down all the initiatives, improvement projects and programmes your company runs. Just the ones you can think of – top of your head. Now sit down and multiply that by three to get a more accurate picture.

While there are many initiatives within the company, there are one or two projects with so much importance within the company (and which cost so much) that they become 'mission critical'. So much time and effort has already been expended that it would be impossible not to continue with them – and they have now taken on a life of their own. Examples I have seen are ERP implementations, Sarbanes-Oxley, outsourcing HR and Six Sigma. They dominate the project sponsor's or project manager's work, who then takes decisions within their programme or initiatives that affect the whole company.

Initiatives move the business forward

In spite of some of the difficulties we have highlighted, initiatives can be successful. They are key to moving the business forward, as major change is not going to happen to the organisation organically. Yet you cannot expect the sales

[1]For 'silo' read function, department, office, fiefdom – whatever your organisational ghetto is called.

force to continue to hit their targets at the same time as implementing a major Customer Management system. You need a dedicated project team to support the initiative.

Many initiatives really do work: they do what they are supposed to do. Everyone will have worked hard to make the business case, and indeed to ensure that their initiative is well planned and rolls out efficiently and effectively.

These initiatives create:

- Improvement ideas

- New ways of organising work

- New structures

- New methodologies

- New software implementation

- Thought leadership

- New, more effective ways of doing things.

They also create a lot of documentation explaining the new working practices and the changes within the new organisation. All of which the workforce need to read, understand and internalise.

A common purpose

How exactly are we going to ensure everyone in the company is aware of the ongoing initiatives and feels ready to apply the relevant part of the 1000s of pages of documentation generated by our initiatives? Considering, in some cases, the initiative is being run by a different department, perhaps in another country?

These initiatives do not add any value at all unless the new ways of working are adopted consistently across the business. Hence $R=IA^2$.

Try to estimate the number of pages generated by your five core initiatives. 500, 1,000, 10,000? How many of those did you read to make sure you apply the ideas in YOUR job?

The issue in large companies running a number of initiatives is that there is no visibility, no way of seeing how they overlap. Therefore the changes from each initiative impact the same departments. Those working in these departments feel like they are hit by waves of change, as the initiatives deliver at different times, and their recommendations are at best inconsistent and often contradictory.

This is not the place for a discussion on Programme Management.[2] I want to focus on the delivery of the results of the projects or initiatives within the programme. Of critical importance is an understanding of the changes in roles and activities as a result of the initiatives. This visibility is not only within the programme, to ensure there is co-ordination, but also into the whole organisation to smooth the roll-out of the changes.

---

[2]This is the discipline of managing multiple projects – rather like herding cats, but with far more at stake.

Chapter 4

Adoption[2]

'It is not necessary to change. Survival is not mandatory.'

Dr W. Edwards Deming,
'Father' of the Quality Movement

What do we mean by adoption?

We call adoption the extent to which the people across your business (including employees, suppliers and contractors) actually do what is required, change to new behaviours, and adopt those behaviours into their everyday working lives consistently and continuously, from the very top to the lowest level of the organisation.

Getting everyone on board is part of it, but it's not just acceptance of a new initiative, it's the integration of it into the day-to-day way of working by everyone in the company, within the context of their work.

It's simple really. No matter how good the initiative you have completed, if no-one changes their way of working, driven by the conclusions of that initiative, it counts for nothing. It doesn't matter how good the output of 'content' is, in whatever form:

- plan
- the 'content' of ideas
- methodologies
- improved systems
- ways of working, etc.

It is the adoption of those ideas that governs the extent to which your objectives will be achieved. I believe that it is far more important to focus the effort on the adoption, rather than the content produced by the initiative. So much so that we put Adoption^2, or Adoption x Adoption, in our formula.

Some questions to consider when launching an initiative that puts the focus on adoption:

- How do you make sure everyone uses the new system so the company gets value from it?

- How do you make sure that disparate projects in different countries become consistent so everyone works at the same level of efficiency?

- How do you make sure that your workforce in country A implements the key characteristics that made country B run with two days' less inventory?

Gaining real adoption

The best laid management plans can result in nothing if your people further down the management chain - the 'adopters' - don't appreciate the bigger picture: the story behind the strategy. There are numerous examples where companies have attempted to initiate the right strategy, only for it never to impact on business processes. Take - for example - the case of an oil refinery, where managers introduced a strategy aimed at cutting costs. They believed the message had got across, but when team members were asked what they considered to be top priorities, they came out with four different answers, none of which was about cutting costs.

Think of all those initiatives you started over the years. I bet those long-standing employees of your company chuckle 'We remember project X. All that time and effort and where did it get us?' Worse still, any new initiatives will be greeted down the line with comments like 'Sounds like project X all over again... I wonder how long this will last?' You have encountered resistance before you even start. It's the opposite of adoption. Everyone will keep their heads down, continue in whatever way they are working, and yet another initiative will indeed have come and gone. Without ever having been really adopted.

Contrast that with an approach where the emphasis is on the way people integrate the new thinking into their day-to-day work and it is not difficult to see why adoption has such an impact.

You've analysed, mapped, benchmarked and finally come up with a new way to procure, supported by a new procurement system; your procurement people immediately start using it as intended. So you get all the benefits promised in the business case. Now that is adoption.

An example

A 360-degree view of customers: 'Customer View'

You are in the middle of implementing a large Customer Relationship Management software solution and the project is called 'Customer View'. I don't have to tell you that you are risking a lot. Potential disruption or even total failure of the project jeopardise not just your key customer relationships but also your future revenue. The reason for the risk is that you need a 360-degree view of your customers, and at the moment that information is held in multiple systems. This means the sales processes, the delivery processes, the order expediting processes and the cash collection processes are convoluted and cumbersome. You've discovered that there are 50 customer touch points within the company.

Therefore the 'Customer View' initiative is going to rationalise and simplify all the customer processes in every area, and tie it all together by holding all the customer data in a single system. That system is Siebel. Siebel is the market leader. It has all the functionality needed by each department and it is infinitely configurable so it can be made to fit the new processes. The only downside is that it requires a team from one of the large System Integrators (SI) to configure it.[1] That means that most of the budget, effort and focus is on the configuration phase. It is a software project.

The project is 18 months long, and the business users have defined what they want. Now they can sit back and wait while the Siebel system is configured and delivered in ten months' time[2]. At that point everyone can be trained.

However, the business will have moved on in the next ten months, and there is little scope to change the Siebel configuration without excruciatingly painful charges from the SI.

Any benefits derived from the new system will come partially from the new way of working and partly because of the access to the customer data. However, the new working practices cannot even be implemented until the new system is in place, so there is an 'opportunity cost' as well as a real cost of software and consultants. Finally, four months is not long to develop training courses, train the staff and bed the system down before the Christmas rush.

Is it any wonder the project manager is going prematurely grey?

Fictitious? Not really - there are probably 100 similar projects in the UK alone. And many of them are massively larger than this.[3]

An alternative approach

An alternative approach - which is almost at the other extreme - comes from a company called salesforce.com, a direct competitor to the likes of Siebel. The salesforce.com application has far less functionality than Siebel, but it addresses the core customer processes. It is hosted by salesforce.com, and, most importantly, it cannot fundamentally be changed, apart from adding a few new fields on each screen, which is a five-minute

[1]That means changing different screens and linking them together into the complete system – a programming job. [2]It is rather like sending a letter to Santa with your wish list (i.e. the requirements), and then waiting until Xmas and hoping he delivers the present you asked for (i.e. the Siebel system). [3]One UK company has had 300 consultants configuring SAP and Siebel for 2 years.

task. So all the effort is spent on understanding how the staff are going to use it. These are all adoption tasks. It is not a software project, but a business change initiative.

The benefits are high adoption, low cost (it costs only around $50 per person per month), and the benefits of the new working practices are implemented in weeks, not months.

The downside is that you may need to simplify and change your processes so that they can use the salesforce.com functionality, rather than change Siebel to exactly how you work. But is this such a bad thing – stacked up against the costs and risks? Couldn't your sales process do with simplifying?

Training people on the new way of working, rather than just on how they should use the new software screens, will get you a long way towards adoption.

Summarising this example, most enterprise applications or custom-written software applications can take man years of systems integration consultants to configure and program. They end up as a major software project, costing millions, with no budget left to drive the change management work to make sure that the business transformation is performed effectively - or, as we say, adopted. The business treated them as 'software implementation projects' not 'business transformation projects' where the software is merely an enabling technology.

Chapter 5

Adoption is achievable

'All truths are easy to understand once
they are discovered.
The point is to discover them.'

Galileo Galilei

The challenge of adoption

By now you are probably asking yourself, 'Is this really possible?' The benefits seem obvious, and the effort of changing the way you approach initiatives seems worth it. The other question that springs to mind is 'How much adoption are we already getting?' Sadly, the answer is probably less than you hoped and far less than the business case for each initiative promised.

However, no matter how large the organisation, adoption is possible. Even if you have 1000, 10,000, 100,000 or even 2 million employees.[1]

So why does it become exponentially difficult as the number of staff increases? The first is that chains of command and communication get longer. The second is that unless everyone is aligned under a common strategy and direction, each initiative/programme/project takes on a life and identity of its own. Each one has sponsors fighting for resources (people and money). People's careers and promotions become dependent on the successful (in their terms) outcome of the project, so this gets in the way of 'doing the right thing for the company'... if indeed they can see what 'doing the right thing for the company' really is.

---

[1] This is a company in China... so if there is a disagreement over strategy and one division decides to go in a different direction it has the same effect as a military coup in a small country. Second thought, they burn up 10,000 man-years of effort EVERY DAY.

I don't believe that most people come into work wanting to do a poor job. They are either badly motivated, badly directed or badly trained.

Adoption starts with a clear message and direction from the top. Clear enough that everyone in the organisation can relate to it. This needs to be something more than the same tired old vision statement of 'To be the leader in blah blah in the next two years. It needs to be something that everyone can relate to in their day job, can remember, and can aspire to. Far better is 'I'm helping to put a man on the moon...'

Man on the moon

The story goes that when President John F. Kennedy was touring the Manned Spacecraft Center at NASA he met a janitor there. When asked what his job was, the janitor answered, 'I'm helping to put a man on the moon.'

I seriously doubt that the head of the Space Agency had someone put together an instruction manual and send out copies to everyone in the space programme detailing the correct answers to such questions. Perhaps he spoke about 'boosting profits and revenue'? Or something along that line. Of course he didn't. What he did do was help people 'see' an astronaut on the moon. And make clear to them that 'we' were going to put him there. The team, every single one of them. Who wouldn't want to be part of an exciting journey like that?

Some companies already take storytelling seriously. 3M, the diversified technology company, for example, trains all its sales representatives to paint stories through word pictures as a means of boosting sales. Storytelling forms a part of 3M's strategic planning, as this is the formal process mapping out the company's route to winning.

What I have seen at the hundreds of companies I have worked with is that the lack of a clear message from the top often leaves staff disorientated and therefore uninterested.

As the *Harvard Business Review* put it in its interview with Robert McKee, one of Hollywood's top scriptwriting consultants: 'Persuasion is the centrepiece of business activity. Customers must be convinced to buy your company's products or services, employees to go along with a new strategic plan or reorganisation, investors to buy (or not to sell) your stock and partners to sign the next deal.'

But adoption is far more than a vision statement, a strong statement from the top, and the CEO appearing at the kick-off meeting. Adoption is about changing people's day-to-day thinking, 'making strategy everybody's day job'. Adoption is required because the results of an initiative require people to change. Remember, $R=IA^2$.

Adoption starts at the top, but it requires an approach which is empathetic to people's fear of change. It is about making change the path of least resistance. Part stick, part carrot.

Adoption in practice – Lockheed Martin

A real-life example is Lockheed Martin in the UK. The results speak for themselves...

- Increase from 450 to 40,000 page views per month of process information on the intranet – clearly showing an increase in adoption

- Contributed significantly to an increase in sales in excess of £30 million

- Giving savings this year of £5.7m and predicted £4.5m next year.

How did they achieve this? The following interview with the head of the change programme gives some insights into the approach and how they delivered such impressive results:

An example

What does Lockheed Martin do?

Lockheed Martin UK-Integrated Systems is recognised as a leader in the design, development and integration of complex systems for defence and commercial markets. Our core capabilities in prime contractorship, systems integration and programme management are strengthened by our ability to enhance existing information investments, maximise system functionality and replace obsolete systems with 'best-of-breed' applications.

This expertise has been applied to several large, complex defence and commercial programmes, while we continue to successfully manage the Merlin programme for the Royal Navy – one of the UK's largest and most sophisticated systems integration projects to date. Other key contracts include the Soothsayer Land Electronic Warfare programme for the British Army and Royal Marines, prime contractor and systems integrator for the Royal Navy's Warship Electronic Chart Display Information System (WECDIS) contract, and our Address Interpretation division is the prime systems integrator for the Royal Mail's SmartStamp online postage service.

What business problem was the IT project attempting to solve?

LM UK-IS sells itself as a prime contractor and systems integrator on large and complex programmes. We aim to consistently deliver sophisticated systems on time and to budget, with low risk and which satisfy the customer's needs. This has always been achieved through rigorous adherence to process, but to stay ahead of the competition we decided to rethink our approach as an enterprise to overcome problems such as:

- Poor responsiveness to process change
- Lack of flexibility in changing to a multi-project company

- Low level of employee engagement in process development and information usage.

The areas affected spanned the entire business, including:

- Business Capture

- Systems Engineering

- Finance

- Corporate Process Management (CPM)

- Risk Management

- Customer Satisfaction Assessment.

What business process change did you implement and why?

Over a planned three-year period we have fundamentally altered our business approach. As a prime contractor we needed a better and more consistent use of business process information to manage ourselves and our more than 200 subcontractors.

The company introduced a top-down total quality management process driven by the executive board and with full buy-in from all stakeholders. We changed from a text-based quality management system to a web-based process mapping and process deployment tool (locally known as the Business Management System, i.e. an IOM[2]).

How did you achieve these impressive results?

All of LM's key business processes (which are of a transactional nature) have been subjected to measured improvement. In addition to a carefully planned mapping of these processes, a monthly TQM Executive Board assesses process performance on a rolling annual programme. An independently verified scorecard called the TQM Practice Assessment Matrix is presented by the responsible Executive Process Owner (2 per month) to the rest of the Board.

[2]Intelligent Operations Manual – all will be revealed in Chapter 7, so be patient.

The scorecard includes process attributes such as customer satisfaction, process investment and training, and improvement plans/achievement. In addition, the company measures its processes against the CMMI (a model for improving and appraising the performance of development organisations) and is planning a major assessment to level 3 in the autumn.

Examples of improved results achieved are:

- The new system automates process authorisation and integrates it with e-mail, making it highly visible and easy to use. **Average days to close corrective actions are down by 75%.**

- By improving access, involvement and presentation, the page views on the new process-mapped information rapidly climbed from a **historical 450 per month to over 40,000 transactions per month**.

- Engaging staff in the processes, their ideas have helped the company to **win more than £30 million of new business,** and save money on existing business.

- Applying rigorous process management has resulted in **actual savings in 2003 of £5.7 million and projected savings of nearly £4.5 million per annum**.

Other tangible process improvement examples:

- Number of steps in the Invoice Payment process down by 70%, saving $2.5 million per annum.

- Customer satisfaction now measured (or planned to be measured) on all projects. Address Interpretation Programme received Silver Award for Customer Satisfaction from the Royal Mail.

- 80% of projects have an approved 67-point process planning sheet which requires planned and tailored processes to be declared (20% in the approval cycle).

- Business Capture Win Rate up from 30% to 100%.

- Average days to close corrective actions are down by 75%.

- Revenue process, projected re-work reduced by 66% (new process still in implementation phase).

- $5 million of smaller process improvement savings banked through the company's 'Cost Effectiveness' suggestion scheme.

- The amount of material has been substantially reduced ('...a picture tells a thousand words....').

Was it more difficult to get these results?

Not really, once we got started. It was a slightly different approach, which took a leap of faith because few other companies had trodden this path. Now it is far less risky.[3]

[3]There is even a book to explain how it was done (this one).

Summary

In summary, Part I of this book has set out what I have defined as (somewhat tongue-in-cheek[1]) the Fundamental Law of Business:

R= IA^2 (Results = Initiatives x Adoption^2)

This formula captures the real essence of what needs to be done to deliver your corporate strategy.

To get those results you've put in place various initiatives to achieve them. The difficulty, in today's dynamic business world, is getting everyone in the organisation to adopt the changes in activity and behaviour to deliver the results and work collaboratively towards the common goals.

Why adoption squared? Adoption has a significantly (hence adoption squared) greater influence. To get better results you should focus on the adoption of the current initiatives, rather than launch more. However, most companies focus their efforts on developing the output of the initiatives (reports, systems, content) while adoption rarely gets formalised and is often left until the initiative is completed and in place rather than woven into the overall initiative from the beginning. Yet adoption is the fundamental requirement for success.

Recognising this means that the effectiveness of your current initiatives can be dramatically improved - and it is within the reach of every one of you. Part II of this book describes how you can solve the Adoption Challenge.

[1] The book is being translated into American (randomly removing the letter U and replacing S with Z) and Chinese. I wonder what the translators will make of this?

PART II: Solving the adoption challenge

Chapter 6

Adoption – The path of least resistance to change

'The definition of insanity is doing the same thing over and over, and expecting different results.'

Benjamin Franklin

6

Pain or pleasure?

Adoption requires people to change; change their behaviours, change their day-to-day activities, change where they sit, change their customs and practices. Effective adoption also puts into context why they need to change and how they can change.

So a clear message from the top gets everyone on 'the same page', pointing in the same direction. But it doesn't get 1000 counter clerks in branch offices applying money laundering checks correctly[1], or outsourced call-centre staff in India applying consistent discounts on new insurance policies, or all the 30 accounts clerks posting transactions correctly to meet Sarbanes-Oxley compliance.

What it requires is a clear, unambiguous statement of what you want someone to do, what tools you want them to use, and what results you want them to get. For every role in the company. For every job. At every level.

 The devil really is in the detail.

For many, change is frightening, even threatening, and therefore it is resisted at all costs. It is that old pain versus pleasure thing. People act to eliminate pain and bring pleasure. Therefore you need to make the new world look more pleasurable than the perceived pain of change. Or you

---

[1] This cost Abbey (leading UK mortgage lender) a £2.3m fine and some unpleasant high-profile publicity recently for not taking proper steps to identify clients for money laundering.

need to make the pain of not changing greater than the pain of the change itself. Either way, make change the path of least resistance.

As managers we need to recognise the effect of the change curve (see illustration, below).

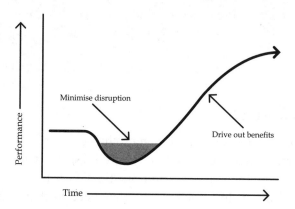

Performance will first drop when a change is adopted. Over time the performance level will rise, and (should) continue to be greater than the previous state. The aim is to reduce the drop in performance and minimise the time to get back above the earlier performance level.

Underpinning any successful change activity is clear communication of what needs to be done, why it is better, how people will be helped through the change and what the new performance measures are.

A study of financial services firms revealed that companies get as little as 20% of the promised pay-off after having completed 80% of the work (of the initiative). The remaining 80% of the benefits comes from dealing with people issues..

Let's see why change management fails, based on a survey by Accenture of senior executives in 14 industries. The survey found that the reasons why a major change initiative was substantially delayed and/or negated were:

- 64% Lack of buy-in that change is necessary
- 44% Lack of skill or experience with change management
- 44% No senior management champion
- 44% Turf battles
- 36% Lack of congruent reward system
- 31% Inability or unwillingness to downsize.

Clearly, people issues are a key part of the problem. The first three reasons show that managers don't want to face up to change or lack the skills or leadership to do it, whereas the bottom three issues seem to point towards deeper concerns in the company culture or HR issues. But they do want the results that the change brings.

The million pound[2] question is: How do you make change successful?

The best way is to see what successful companies do – companies that survive and thrive on radical change. First of all, everyone involved understands that change happens and things need to change. Secondly, there is someone clearly leading the process and the strategy. Everyone buys into the change and understands the critical reasons it needs to happen. The company is actually capable of change (there is the capability and ability to change, learn and innovate over time). And most importantly, it does not happen overnight. There is no such thing as 'instant change'. Successful change management is stubborn, persistent and consistent.

Change strategies

By now, you've probably realised that change is not one-size-fits-all. Every organisation, based on its culture, maturity and market conditions, will need to address change in a different way to ensure that the desired results are achieved. The type of change can be analysed by considering

---

[2]This is the $64,000 question adjusted for inflation. It is probably a question with a far larger price tag for most of you.

three different factors.

- Speed: How important is speed to accomplishing the objectives of the change effort? Is the pace determined by the markets, the competition or the customers?

- Conformance: How closely must we follow the specific processes or outcome to achieve our goals? Is there regulatory pressure to conform or would it stifle innovation?

- Commitment: How important is it to ensure that everyone in the organisation understands the need for change and is prepared to do what it takes?

If you then consider the relative importance of each of these three factors together, you identify the most appropriate change strategy, as we have shown in the following diagram.[3]

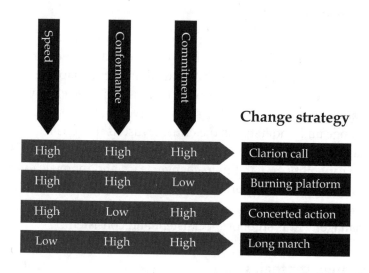

Speed	Conformance	Commitment	Change strategy
High	High	High	Clarion call
High	High	Low	Burning platform
High	Low	High	Concerted action
Low	High	High	Long march

Clarion call: Requires that the change is driven by senior management leadership who show a strong commitment to the change. This is because the need and speed for change are not apparent further down the organisation.

[3]Taken from a presentation during the 'Inspiring Performance' Conference, London given by Peter Cheese, Accenture in 2004.

Burning platform: Everyone already recognises the need for change. Therefore a clear message about what is required to change is needed. The risk is that the actions from different parts of the organisation (in their panic) are uncoordinated and inconsistent.

Concerted action: This requires delegation of the change so that it can be applied autonomously throughout the organisation. Yet it still requires the changes to fit within the overall business strategy.

Long march: A long-term initiative which has a strong identity and clear sponsorship from the top so that there is continued commitment to the change. No-one loses sight of the end goal. It also requires clear metrics to show that the changes are working.

Each strategy has its own attributes, but all of them demand a consistent communication of what is required both down and across the organisation. Clearly, the urgency and tone of that communication varies.

What is common in these strategies is the need for every part of the organisation to have a shared understanding of what is required of them. The communication that is required is not a 'weekly email from the CEO'. The communication needs to cover who needs to change, what behaviours need to change, what day-to-day activities will be different, what organisational or reporting structures have changed, and what physical changes need to happen. But to be able to get adoption and buy-in to the change, that communication also needs to put into the context of both why the change is needed and of the expected results of the change – i.e. why it will be better.[4]

Change is not confined to the lowest levels of the organisation. Often the most resistance to change is in the senior management and middle management levels, which is why a transparent, top-down approach is required.

---

[4]Even if it may not be better for some individuals, all of the time.

The key to adoption and buy-in of any change strategy is involvement and communication consistently around the organisation across disciplines (Finance, Logistics, R&D, Manufacturing, Customer Facing, IT) and at every level (CEO, CFO, Divisional Heads, Department Heads, Managers, Accounts Clerks, Warehousemen, Call-centre staff).

This is potentially the most complex information to convey, and a common language is required. This common language is about operations (doing things) and therefore about processes. It needs to support the lowest common denominator – the person who is least adept at understanding it.[5]

An example

Moving to a process-orientated culture within the automotive industry

The major merger of two significant automotive brands resulted in a far more complex organisation that demanded clearer processes to succeed. The UK Board wanted to review its internal quality management system in order to move towards a more process-orientated approach supported by a common operational view. Other key factors to address involved empowering line managers with the tools and knowledge, first to define and ultimately to manage their processes independently, and this required adoption across the entire organisation.

They required an intranet-accessed system to capture the organisation's business processes for accreditation and to allow all employees across the company to use the processes on a daily basis. This would also allow immediate feedback to process owners on any issues concerning the quality and effectiveness of the company's processes for continual improvement and development – through the intranet.

[5]Probably the CEO.

The results were that they developed a 'living' process knowledge base which had improved competitive advantage and customer service. The continuous improvement programme gained ISO compliance and the approach enabled performance targets to be assigned to key processes. The IOM has gone on to be extended to capture, define and improve the processes associated with customer facing activities, where it is recognised that process excellence results in sustainable competitive advantage and a delighted customer.

Chapter 7

A common language and platform

'England and America are two countries divided by a common language.'

George Bernard Shaw, playwright

We need a common language

Effective change requires a consistent communication of what is required of individuals. As most of that communication is about what they should do differently, and that is often complex, a common language is required. A language that everyone understands, whatever their position in the company and wherever they are located. Something global, something inclusive. All those divisions of your company, do they speak the same language? Are Production baffled by the jargon and acronyms used by IT, and vice versa?

That language needs to consider where the communication breakdown is.

Is it, in the case of a major software implementation, in the definition/configuration phase between the project team users and the IT team who are configuring the new system? The business areas are describing how they want to work, and the IT team are describing the data and screen designs.

Or is it in the roll-out/training phase between the project team users, who have lived and breathed the new world for months, and the end users who are being trained on the data entry screens of the new system with no context of how this fits with their new roles?

They are all trying to convey the same information – how the business is going to operate in the new world. What are the new processes in context, what are the new forms and screens, how are the new policies going to be applied, what are the new rules?

The common language needs to be shared across the business disciplines because all core processes are not confined to those silos. The terminology that is now being used says it all – Order to Cash, Idea to Product, Recruit to Retire. These are end-to-end processes. Often these will span multiple countries or offices. The teams of people may be pooled in 'Shared Service Centres' or be part of another company as they are outsourced. But the customer expects a seamless delivery.[1]

Finally, it needs to be a language of operations – activities, performance, tasks – action-oriented. And it needs to be able to cater for complex paths and ad-hoc tasks, not just the neatly ordered activities. This language is composed more of pictures than of words.

Interestingly, the building blocks of this language have been around for years in the form of process maps. Unfortunately, each area of the business has complicated them by adding their interpretation and meaning to the diagrams and by adding their own notation. In a way the language has gained its own dialect – so it is no longer common.

In addition, the processes have been put in the language of the business analyst – with huge, detailed flow charts describing the intricate detail of an activity or task. But it cannot be put in the wider context so that the supervisor or senior manager can understand it or use it. Certainly a CEO or CFO would not recognise it, so there is a clear divide between those who have set the strategy and those who are delivering it. In many ways this divide is greater and more damaging than the infamous 'Business/IT divide'.

[1] As a customer, why should I care how you are organised or distributed?

Can you identify a common language of operation in your organisation? Is it just words or pictures?

This common language may need to be imposed, and then its simplicity protected. It cannot be modified for each different group of users – because it won't be a common language. The language is shared and owned by everyone.

This language ultimately needs to describe the entire operation of the company. For every role in the company. For every job. At every level. Before we get too far, we need to understand its audience. To understand the audience and why they need to see this information will give some insights into how it should be presented.

The CEO – needs to set strategy, needs to see a clear picture of the handoffs and responsibilities of each department, needs a view of how each area is performing, organised as scorecards and also in the context of the activities.

The departmental manager – needs to see a clear picture of the handoffs and responsibilities of each team, needs a view of how each area is performing, organised as scorecards and also in the context of the activities.

The IT project manager – needs to understand the business flows to be able to configure or fine-tune the software applications, and needs to be able to sign off business changes.

The call centre operative – needs to have an interactive training manual, needs to be confident that the information is correct, and needs to have a reference point for unusual situations.

The outsource delivery manager – needs to be able to work with outsource vendors to optimise processes, and needs to have evidence that the outsource partner is hitting targets (SLAs).

Everyone can use a common language

The language they will share is described in what I have called the Intelligent Operations Manual – IOM.

Years ago companies had operations manuals lovingly cared for by Quality Managers. They fell into disrepute as they were unread, except prior to the annual ISO 9000 audit. Now with a connected PC on every desk, in every briefcase and in every pocket, it is time to reinvent the 'operations manual'.

The scope of the IOM eventually covers the whole company where there could be literally hundreds of activities described on hundreds of diagrams. These can be arranged hierarchically underneath a single diagram which describes the company. Each of the activities on that diagram can be broken down to the next level of detail, in context. This continues all the way down, possibly four to five levels, until you get to the activities that are actually performed.

At any level performance metrics can be attached, links to useful information (websites, policy documents, screen shots, applications). This is the 'single source of truth' about the operation of the business. As I said earlier, the devil is in the detail. You have to get down to this level to make any difference, as it is here that activities are performed differently. The higher levels are important as they enable the managers to understand the context, hand-offs and performance of the processes so that they can make the correct decisions.

Fundamentally the IOM ensures that each of the strategic initiatives is consistent, and is taking the whole business forward holistically. It encourages adoption. It certainly gives you a better chance than the 1000 or so pages produced by consultants you are expected to read – alongside your day job.[2]

---

[2] I asked one client about their customer order process and was told that it had been documented. He went to a filing cabinet and proudly produced a 58-page textual document with some flow charts amongst the text.

So the IOM enables you to:

- Define each individual's role, responsibility and accountability.

- Measure and gain visibility of end-to-end process, throughout the organisation.

- Proactively audit conformance to company and regulatory requirements.

- Actively promote collaboration between departments, functions and individuals.

The IOM is the shared picture of the company's operations – so we need to agree corporately on how it should look in terms of layout, structure, colours and styles. This is KEY. It is not enough to have your IT staff conduct interviews to find out what 'we (the users) want' and for them to decide what suits them. This is about end-user engagement and is fundamental to this approach. It is used to create and maintain the IOM, so that you get downstream adoption. More of this in Part IV.

What happens if you take a wrong turn

A global telecommunications company has invested in some tools to document their business in terms of process. They bought over 600 licences and have spent hundreds of man-years putting 400 process models into the repository (process database). The project manager commented that this was a WRITE ONLY database, i.e. nobody reads it.

The root cause is that the process team, a separate body, are the people who maintain the process information in the repository. So would the rest of the company read it? It's not theirs. They have no ownership as they weren't really involved or engaged in the creation of the materials. The tool was too complex and designed for the trained business analyst, so was not designed for end users. Also, the language used to describe the processes was too complex, too rich, and too specific to be comprehensible to end users.

Clearly this is NOT adoption. Interestingly, the successes cited by the Project Manager were all internal successes, and did not appear to impact their bottom line. These benefits included:

- Productivity doubled in Process Team
- Reduction in paper documentation
- Increased professionalism for business consultants.

Invisible asset

However, by taking a different, proven approach for building the IOM you can make it READ/WRITE. Then it becomes an asset for the initial initiative that established it, but is also a very valuable asset for the whole company moving forward.

The IOM is the key asset that you never had, and you never really missed until that Sarbanes-Oxley audit, or that product recall due to incorrectly labelled product.[3]

So where does all this information currently lie? Mostly in the employees' heads, and it walks out of the door every evening, or out of the company forever when part of the company is made redundant. In some areas that knowledge is particularly short-lived, for example in call centres where the staff turnover is over 100%, and there is a perpetual training effort to bring new people up to speed.

Surely it is embedded in SAP, Oracle, PeopleSoft – or whatever software application we installed? That's what the salesman said and the brochure claimed. That is where the processes are run.

Surely it has been captured in the workflow solution which we spent millions implementing?

[3]Suddenly CEOs, keen to avoid prison, are becoming interested in Sarbanes-Oxley compliance.

The answer is yes and no.

Certainly parts of the process are defined in the systems, but not all of it. They define only the interaction of the processes with the screens and the data entry.

Relying on just the systems means that people do not have the manual processes defined, and they do not have the context to understand how to use the system/screens. This can result in inconsistent data being entered into the system.

An insurance company in Thailand has this problem, and has it magnified. Their system has all the field names, which describe what data should be entered, in English. Therefore the local Thai workforce, who do not understand English, have only folklore passed from worker to worker to describe the use of the system. The result is that the data entered into each field varies from worker to worker.

Using the IOM brings both the people-based processes and system-supported processes together and also brings the metrics/performance data and puts it into context. Traditionally the metrics are divorced from the processes that create or affect the metrics. Mad, but true.

So why would people refer to the IOM? Probably for five reasons:

- they are new to the company and are being trained

- they want to see how their processes are performing

- they want to brush up on a process with which they are unfamiliar

- they want to suggest some improvements and kick off a change

- they have been notified of a change to a standard process.

So what does this IOM look like?

Please don't skip over this piece as you think you have seen it all before, saying 'It's all boxes and lines...we do that'.

Just because it looks like a box on one of your flow charts, the way is it described and the attributes are critical. Take a moment to look at the picture, and see if you can work out why this is pretty useless.

This is just a box which does not describe an action. It's just an organisation with no defined inputs or outputs.

But this works...

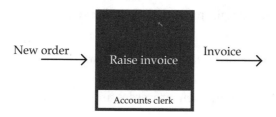

It has some important attributes. Firstly it is action-oriented.

- The words in the box are 'raise invoice', not some organisation 'accounts'.

- The activity is triggered by something ('new order') and results in something ('invoice'). Many diagrams we see have no input or output. How do we know when the activity starts or finishes. This is the critical 'hand off'.

- The person accountable for the process (the accounts clerk) is named.

Let's now add some supporting information so that this becomes useful on a daily basis as the 'single source of truth'.

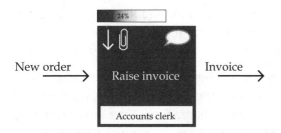

- The 'drill down arrow' (top left corner of the box) indicates that that there is a lower-level set of activities which describe this activity in more detail. There is a hierarchy of interconnected diagrams, so the user is not swamped with detail.[4]

- The 'document' (the paper clip icon) shows that there are some links to supporting information, such as links to the Oracle Accounts Invoice screen, screen shots showing how to complete the Invoice screen, the current price list and the invoicing policy document. No more searching for related information, or doubts about its validity.

- The 'notes bubble' (top right of box) shows there may be some hints and tips for this activity.

- Finally, the 'performance status bar' (just above the main box) shows how well this activity is being conducted. It could easily be displayed as a traffic light. There is a link to the systems that produced the data to allow further investigation to understand why the performance is not at 100%. Maybe you could look 'upstream' to see whether the poor performance is due to inaccurate orders?

---

[4] I've been shown process diagrams that, when printed out, span three walls of a project office with thousands of activities. These proved impenetrable even for the consultants who wrote them – much to their embarrassment in front of the client.

Two simple principles which make all the difference

The secret of this approach is that two key principles are applied to every diagram, at whatever level in the IOM.

Firstly, every diagram in the IOM is built up using these simple constructs. Therefore there is a common language between top management and the shopfloor, between finance and logistics. This ensures that there is effective communication.

There are no special notations for the top-level diagram, for the 'context diagram', for the Level 1 diagram, for the Level 4 diagram and so on. Every diagram uses the same structure, as it can be used to show extremely complex flows with multiple branches and ad-hoc activities.

The second principle is that there are no more than 6–10 activity boxes on a diagram. Any more than that and it becomes too crowded, and unreadable on a PC screen. Projects that proudly display diagrams covering the walls of the 'war room' are sadly missing the point. The reason for creating these diagrams is to share the information.

Put another way . . .

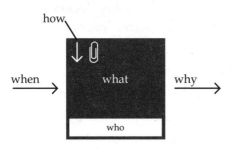

Keeping it readable

The way to keep the diagrams simple is to take the detail and 'force it down a level'. That means that the detailed activities (which describe the higher-level activity), are documented in a diagram which is the 'child' of the activity. This means that there is a parent-child relationship between the diagrams. This can happen multiple times so that you are building a hierarchy of diagrams, all of which are readable.[5]

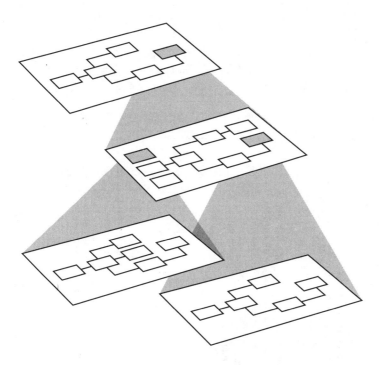

The beauty of this approach is that you can see the context before you 'drill down', and therefore you are not swamped with detail. This means that the diagrams are far more 'approachable', and this encourages adoption. If an end user is confronted with a complex jargon-filled diagram with multiple boxes they will run a mile, and they are more likely to ask a colleague about their role or make it up. Consistency flies out of the window.

[5]The largest hierarchy I've seen started with a top-level diagram of eight activity boxes, under which there were 6000 diagrams. This described the entire operation of a telecommunications company.

Example diagram in an IOM

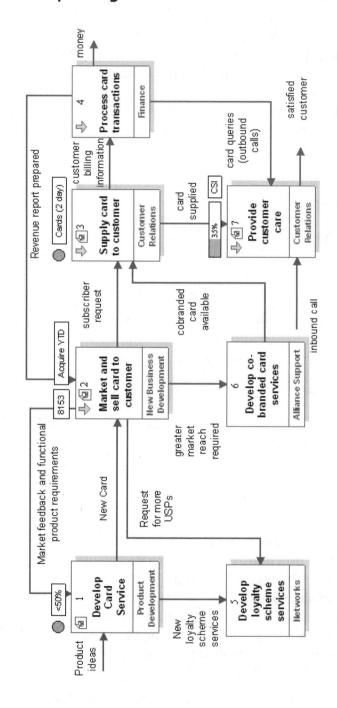

Building an IOM that engenders adoption

Apply the basic building block consistently. Build simple, readable diagrams by structuring them into a hierarchy.

These are the key messages when developing the IOM which will be owned and accessed by everyone in the organisation. There are a few more secrets to gaining adoption and I'll reveal these in Part IV.

Chapter 8

Numbers vs process

'Of the two evils we should choose the least.'

Erasmus (1465–1536)

Business performance in numbers

Performance in business these days (and for the foreseeable future, I would imagine) is usually defined in budget discussions, then measured and reported by your Finance Department and for publicly quoted companies reported to the City. The Finance Department will of course liaise with the business functions/divisions to put together the budget, and (where the data is not collected automatically in some system) gather reporting figures.

The blatant misreporting of figures by a number of companies over the last few years has shown that the numbers don't tell the whole story. They describe the results of actions however inconsistent, flawed or manipulated those actions may have been.

So endemic is the perceived problem of reporting that the Sarbanes-Oxley Act has been passed which forces top management to sign that the numbers have been produced correctly. This means that they must have confidence in the way the numbers have been produced.[1]

You could say that the numbers are the one common language in business, but as a common operational language the numbers on their own are just not enough. The IOM draws together both the activities and the numbers.

[1] So much confidence they are willing to bet their job on it.

Linking processes and metrics

Think about this: top management defines company goals and strategy and takes the lead on a number of key major initiatives. They will have defined the 'Critical Success Factors' (CSF) and will have outlined a budget. I am sure they will have included the Key Performance Indicators (KPI) so that the finance department can measure and assess the result. The people in charge of operations translate the efforts to be made into operational processes and this runs down the hierarchical chains of the company.

Yet the problem is that in many companies the two activities of (a) the definition of Key Performance Indicators and (b) translating them into operational processes to make it all happen, are not linked. Each goes its own way.

As a consequence, the people in the finance department (who are doing all the work to prepare the budgets, deliver management reports and so on) have few links to what is really happening, and, conversely, the people in the operational end of the company probably have no understanding as to how their actions help in actually realising those budgets.

Enter the common operational language, where strategy gets translated from the top down in an uncomplicated way by defining processes linked to performance metrics. Whenever there are questions about how to do things (the operational people), or how well things are getting done (the finance people), anyone can have a look at the tools that have been used to record and describe these processes and find the most up-to-date information.

Corporate Performance Management

What I have described is sometimes called Corporate Performance Management, Business Performance Management or Enterprise Performance Management, i.e. the principle of displaying metrics and associated processes so that the overall performance of the business can be monitored and improved.

However, some IT analysts (such as Gartner) started off with a data- or metrics-centred view of performance management. Their view of performance management consisted of fixing the planning and reporting cycle. Currently, in most businesses, this is a series of MSExcel spreadsheets which are distributed throughout the organisation. This is being replaced by Planning systems for the budgeting cycle, and Business Intelligence and Scorecarding systems for reporting.[2]

What analysts are now recognising, driven by clients voicing their needs, is that there is a process element required to get the full picture. The previous metrics-only view is not really Corporate Performance Management, but Corporate Performance *Reporting*. There is no ability to change, as there is no relationship to process – the things that people really do.

No surprise, then, that many of the Business Intelligence software vendors are now looking at how they add process management to their Corporate Performance management suites of software. I believe that this is more likely to be by acquisition or through strategic partnerships rather than internal development, as the Business Intelligence vendors' world and expertise is in the management and manipulation of vast quantities of data. They have no experience managing processes in the form of interrelated diagrams and their linked documents and applications. Combine this with the management of multiple versions and compliance and you have a complex problem.

[2]This is not surprising as the Business Intelligence vendors are using their marketing budgets to drive the definition of CPM.

What comes first: metrics or process?

Based on the understanding that both process and metrics are needed to complete the IOM, then which comes first? This is a pertinent question as there are many companies which already have scorecarding initiatives that are defining metrics.

So what exactly do I mean by metrics?

You have a company which develops, manufactures and sells electronic equipment. Part of the strategy says that you need new product development to produce five new products, each with a minimum of £30 million sales each year by the third year as a Critical Success Factor (CSF).

The metric here is the number of new products with a minimum of £30 million sales per year.

Therefore the underpinning Key Performance Indicators (KPI) in the six-stage product development process include:

- 20 new ideas at stage two
- budget tolerance up to 5% at stage four
- product approval sign-off process to take less than 30 working days in stage six.

This gives you a hierarchy of interlinked measures, so that people at every level in the company understand their responsibilities and have clear accountability.

 People act as they are measured.

So, if you believe the Business Intelligence software vendors, just install their software and start measuring things for which you have data. This is because their software is good at aggregating all the corporate data and presenting it in a meaningful way – as reports or scorecards. However, this is not as valuable as working out what you should be measuring and going to find that data.

Once people start being measured they will start to change

their behaviour. This is human nature. Over time areas of poor performance will be identified and, in analysing the processes that are broken, you need to make improvements in the processes. This requires people to change – for a second time. You will also begin fully to understand the measures, associated with the new processes, that you really want to hold people accountable for.

So this demonstrates that the metrics-first approach requires people to change twice – once as you start, and then once again as you implement improvements.

However, a process-led approach starts with an analysis of the operational processes. This reinforces the strategic direction from the top. At the highest level you define the core processes and the corresponding measures. Both the process and the metrics are broken down hierarchically, level by level, at the same time.

The act of discovering the processes helps you simplify them and improve them. At each level the metrics reinforce the new processes. Therefore change is only needed once and it is supported by shared access and adoption of the IOM.

 If getting people to change is difficult, then changing twice in a relatively short space of time is more than TWICE as difficult.

Chapter 9

Why now?

'There will never be more than a million cars on Earth – there will never be enough chauffeurs.'
Gottlieb Daimler, 1890
[co-founder of the Mercedes-Benz group]

Intelligent Operations Manual is not really new

The Intelligent Operations Manual is all about bringing no-nonsense business principles back into the boardroom. The high-flying days of $30 million venture capital cheques for six PowerPoint slides to launch a website that sells goldfish with different coloured eyes are a thing of the past. Today's business world is a cautious one where the business model is more likely to resemble the day-to-day dependability of the corner shop than the promised land of e-everything in the 1990s.

What I am talking about is not a new fad – it is more an approach based firmly on a set of business principles that have been around for a long time. The wise old sage says, 'Be concerned with creating a good business model. Be concerned with consistency. Be concerned with making a good product. Keep your feet on the ground. Keep your finger on the pulse of the market and your competition. Keep your eye on the bottom line. Or in other words, KISS. Keep it simple, stupid.'

Unfortunately, KISS is a bit of a silly acronym to sum up a business practice, but one must admit that compared to getting lost in the onslaught of MRP, ERP, CRM, SOA, BPR, BI, BPM, EAI and EOA (Every Other Acronym), KISS is a rather refreshing idea. After all of this ERP-hype, it is high time to 'get back to basics'. The real basics: doing business.

This 'back to basics' is being called performance management, and it is suddenly getting a lot of coverage. Clearly, the principles of this book are at the heart of performance management. Why now, if it is not new and is so obvious?

There are four reasons why performance management is timely, and major corporations around the world are picking up on the principles detailed in this book:

- a focus on simplification and getting a clearer understanding of the business

- the communication and collaboration power of the internet/intranet

- a PC or laptop on every desk or in every briefcase

- affordable software specifically designed to develop and maintain an IOM.

Simplification

Businesses are striving, due to competitive pressures, to drive out cost and time over every process. This is making them re-evaluate their core end-to-end processes, breaking down the silo-thinking[1] that hampered them. They challenge every activity to establish whether it is critical to the core process, and at the same time identify the KPIs that will be used to judge the process.

Along with this simplification is the automation of core processes by implementing (or upgrading) enterprise software. These solutions cover accounting, procurement, personnel, logistics, etc. Alternatively, Business Process Management Systems (BPMS) can be used to automate activities by stitching together various existing applications or by designing custom-workflow applications.

A measure of the recent activity is that SAP, which already has a revenue of $5 billion, has seen a software licence

[1] Design engineers, when designing cars, may spend little time thinking about the maintenance of that vehicle. Take the example where the clutch needs to be changed after 30,000 miles and, to do so, the engine has to be taken out. It's not their problem...

increase of 25% this year. The BPMS market is starting to consolidate, as there are currently over 200 suppliers in this arena. From this group some clear winners will emerge who have global reach and the capability to support Fortune 500 companies.[2]

The internet

It has become obvious that the internet is not a business in its own right, but an enabling technology. It has dramatically reduced the cost and complexity of providing global communication of information throughout a company. It offers the same end user experience if they are sitting at their desk, in a café, at a client site or at home.[3]

Not only is that information available, but it can also be kept up to date real-time. This, and its universality, allows genuine collaboration to work.

A couple of companies that have proven the value of the communication and collaboration are eBay, the world's largest on-line car boot sale, and Friends Reunited, a website which allows school and college friends to communicate. Neither could have existed cost-effectively without the internet. The same is true for the internal communications within companies. Virtually every major company has an intranet which links multiple office locations and can be accessed by remote workers. An intranet is no longer Competitive Advantage, it is mandatory.

The internet has made possible the idea of the IOM being the 'single source of truth', linked to external systems, documents and data. Not only is secure access possible by office-based and remote workers, but they have confidence that the information is current.

As the CFO of a multinational building company said of his site-based teams, 'I don't want them ever to have the excuse that they didn't know what to do.'

The internet means that the IOM can be made available

---

[2]Picking a workflow vendor for a strategic area of the business isn't easy. You may not like SAP's pricing, but at least you know they will be around in the next couple of years. [3]If only the same could be said for the quality of the coffee.

outside the company, with rights controlling what can and can't be seen. Why shouldn't your re-sellers see where they fit into your customer order process, access the latest data sheets and price lists held on your servers, and have access to scorecards that monitor their performance?

Your suppliers are an integral part of your supply chain. They are often the key customer touch point. Therefore, it is even more critical that they are tightly bound into your end-to-end processes. Giving them access to the IOM, involving them in reviews and electronically notifying them of changes will mean that they can act as if they are part of the company. Adoption is even harder here, yet just as critical. Adoption is important if they are supplying component parts for you. It is critical if they are installing phone equipment in your customers' homes.

When you make changes to business processes, you brief the internal team. But who will make sure the outsourced call centre staff are up to speed, bearing in mind that staff turnover (churn) can be as high as 90%?

PC on every desk

Bill Gates had a vision of a computer in every home. Even he underestimated it. I'm sitting here and I can see three PCs, not counting the web capability of my mobile phone and my PDA. In the office it is no different. Every executive has a laptop in his briefcase and every knowledge worker has a PC on his desk. Even companies with staff working away from the office in hazardous conditions are equipping them with a PDA to provide access to current information. It is no longer a question of hardware investment. Today, it is almost ironic that the software rights for Microsoft's OS are more expensive than the server itself.[4] The infrastructure is clearly there, which has made the deployment of the IOM to everyone in the organisation possible at virtually no cost. All that is required is intranet or internet access and a device that can view web pages.

---

[4]Especially when you consider that Bill Gates is one of the richest men in the world. It is a clear indication of a software monopoly at work and that there are still strong market forces in hardware.

Affordable software

To make the IOM possible, you need software designed to develop and manage it. This can be done with existing software tools such as MSOffice. It can even be done with paper. But neither approach is seamless or easy enough to be sustainable. Remember we need the IOM to remain the 'single source of truth' long after the initiative that created it has gone.

 To get people to do something it needs to be simple, easy and friendly.[5]

Only ten or 15 years ago software needed to be designed for a specific network and database and to be driven by a mainframe. Access was via the Local or Wide Area Network. The software was complex, had custom-written interfaces with other systems and consequently was difficult to write – and hence expensive.

Software can now be far simpler, using the internet as the communication vehicle for end users to access the information, for collaboration, and for getting information from other systems.

Software can even be licensed in a number of more creative ways to be able to reduce the upfront cost and therefore allow companies to pilot the approach. The software could be hosted by the software vendor so there is no impact on the client's systems. It could be licensed on a per usage basis – the more adoption you get, the more the IOM is accessed, the higher the fee.[6]

My experience is that pilot schemes can deliver remarkable results so that a very robust business case for full roll-out can be generated. Think back to $R=IA^2$. If this approach and the IOM improves the adoption for one initiative, then it has paid for itself. Subsequent initiatives can piggyback on the work for an even lower cost.

[5] Or, if none of these, massively well paid.
[6] Something we've called 'Pay as You Grow'.

The time is now

Charles Handy's *The Empty Raincoat* mentions that when asking directions for a pub in Ireland, he was told to keep on going straight, straight all the way, and then take a right up a hill. Upon driving off without a second thought to this illogical array of directions, he summed it up perfectly as a paradox for our times:

'By the time you know where you ought to go, it's too late to go there; or more dramatically, if you keep on going the way you are, you will miss the road to the future.'

Handy has identified the time to start working on the next new project or new idea – at the point when positive energy is still good or, even better, fantastic. You want to start when people are motivated and enthused – not at the end of a project or process when mood and activity goes downhill. Unfortunately, in most organisations, this is the only time when the moment is ripe for change – time for a new initiative to motivate everyone, or at worst when the entire company is looking disaster smack in the face.

It has to be said, though, that it is often easier to get action when standing on the edge of the precipice.

So the time is now. There are companies proving the benefits of the IOM, the infrastructure (hardware and communications) is in place, and the software to make it easy to get going is now affordable.

Chapter 10

The benefits of leveraging the IOM

'That's it baby, when you've got it, flaunt it.'

Mel Brooks

Benefits of the IOM from the very first initiative

Clearly there are compelling business cases developed prior to the launch of initiatives in the company. That is why the Board or sponsor sanctioned them. The business case is dependent on a reasonable level of adoption of the findings or results of the initiative. I bet that they were probably based on 100% adoption either because the concept of adoption was never considered or because 100% was needed to make the business case work.

The first initiative in which you apply this adoption approach will immediately establish the value of the IOM and put in place the basic structure and operation.

Yet putting the IOM in place adds little to the cost side of the initiative's business case. As several of our case studies show, there is less, not more, work, particularly in the early process definition phases to build the IOM. It is significantly less time-consuming (and therefore costs less) than the traditional approach of interviews and documentation using MSOffice. It is much quicker to produce the information that builds the IOM as this is done through live workshops, which ensures immediate consensus in the room and the more rapid gaining of agreement to the processes.

Its very structure and the graphic nature of the IOM means that the end user only needs to look at one diagram or screen at a time that is directly relevant. Added to that, the IOM is available to everyone, and because it is accessible, unambiguous and easy to understand, this reinforces adoption.

The communication of the IOM is through the intranet, which is already established in most companies so there is no additional infrastructure cost. The only additional cost is the licensing of software to develop and maintain the IOM.

The benefits of adoption, i.e. delivering the results of the initiative declared in the business case, provide the justification for putting the IOM in place in the first instance.

An example

One million customers

Background

A multinational communication networks and services company enables businesses of all sizes to achieve superior results. More than 90% of the Fortune 500 rely on the company every day and it has offices in 40 countries.

Their IT systems include a highly customised version of SAP for the domestic US operation and a variety of ERP packages throughout the rest of the world. When they originally configured SAP to meet the company's needs they took a 'traditional' approach, taking 200 stakeholders offsite for a week to build a 'to-be' model of the required operation using flip-charts, whiteboards and workshops. This resulted in a textual business requirements specification.

An aggressive project deadline was set. As the deadline approached, the scope of the agreed changes was limited. As the business requirements specification was textual it was difficult to assess the true impact of abandoned or altered functionality. The deadline was met, but for three months the business was compromised as cracks appeared – they couldn't write an invoice. Why? Because despite the fact that individual elements passed user acceptance and testing, it was impossible to see the end-to-end processes.

A catalyst for change

Two years later, the CEO launched an initiative to transform the performance of the 'quote to cash' process globally and to automate the resultant process with an upgraded ERP/CRM solution based on vanilla SAP and Siebel. Customisation would be limited and any changes would need approval at the highest level: the company's CEO.

The key motive was to adapt their business processes to make the most of SAP and Siebel's existing 'out of the box' functionality, configured but not customised. Defining processes that met their vision and business objectives, focused around the needs of customers, while working within the technology constraints, required fundamental changes. The challenge thrown down by the CEO was to rollout in 18 months.

The SAP 'quote to cash' process in the non-US business was documented in an IOM and it became apparent that it could be a major enabler of process visualisation and collaborative development. The Business Transformation project team could see that the traditional approach was not going to deliver in the time, so they took the decision to base the workshop methodology and the business process design on the IOM.

And what an impact it made

Senior Management bought into the vision, but needed quick results to drive visibility and gain momentum. Within three weeks the workshops were up and running. Two weeks later the core 'quote to cash' business processes were captured and collaboratively agreed across the US, Europe and Asia Pacific.

They were able to drive the capture of the entire core process from workshops hosted in the US but with participation from three continents, all developing content live into the IOM which was on a server in the UK. At the same time, stakeholders and workshop participants around the world were able to log-in through their browsers and provide collaborative input and agreement from their local desktops.

When the System Integrator (SI) was selected, their business and systems analysts were able to contribute to the iterative process by showing how SAP and Siebel best practices could support the business processes, and where processes would need to change to fit the functionality available. In terms of implementing SAP and Siebel, this meant that the resultant processes were already known and bought into by BOTH the business users and the technical analysts who were defining the way that SAP/Siebel would be configured. This clarity significantly de-risked the implementation phases. It ensured the process implications of these changes were understood and planned for long before the phased releases. The IOM they now had gave a 360° view of the impact of process change on systems and system upgrades on process.

As the releases were phased and the processes evolved over an 18-month period, there was a picture of 'how the business works' for each phase of the implementation. This provided the 'To Be' fully documented design of the business, on everyone's desktop, in a managed, compliant environment. The implications on adoption rates, training, impact analysis and change management were huge.

One week into the 'quote to cash' workshop, the benefits of the workshop approach and the IOM were so obvious that the decision was made to adopt the same approach for other strands of the business, including the vital area of Service Delivery. Within two months the business transformation benefits were so clear, it had become the global standard.

The following interview with the Head of Business Transformation gives some insights into the project:

What is the IOM delivering that wasn't present before?

Firstly, it provides the mechanism and vocabulary for business people to define what they want to do in clear, unambiguous terms. With the technical people onhand, live, participating in the process workshop, they can show how SAP and Siebel can either support the activities, or how the activities will have to change to fit what the technology can do. The IOM enables us to capture all the business requirements needed for SAP and Siebel implementation in the context of specific activities. This means we can conduct rapid analyses on the impact of release changes, slippage of specific SAP or Siebel modules and see the effect of that on the processes we will have to operate.

Where has the IOM added value?

There is untold value in the process-led environment. High-level process identification allows us to translate the vision of the leadership team into a tangible set of business processes right down to transactional level, ensuring that activities are aligned with high-level objectives. If a process isn't aligned to customer and corporate needs, it's a source of dissatisfaction for everyone and an overhead to the business.

All employees will have access to consistent, sustainable, and repeatable processes in a hierarchical, graphical web-based format. Their roles have also become better defined. Instructor-led training will be reduced and the processes link directly into the applications at transaction level.

This means that the IOM becomes the 'glue' that unifies business needs, system solutions, transactional process performance and accountability of the people who operate and manage those processes. Also, we have a system that is ISO 9000 compliant. And in the wake of high-profile US corporate scandals, 'Sarbanes-Oxley' is the set of US laws governing new codes of business practice. Unsurprisingly, these new laws require controls based around consistent, documented and applied process.

Can you identify some key lessons learned?

- Get the approach agreed and documented before you start workshops, especially if using a Systems Integrator.

- Be strong about using the methodology. Everyone in the workshop including the System Integrators (SI) will need to get their heads around the methodology and may offer their own (different) view of how it should be done. Show the SI how their needs can be serviced and make sure that this is in their contract.

- Initially SI may be taken aback by a customer who knows exactly what they want, but they will quickly become enthused by the jump-start it gives.

- In terms of driving the capture of good content, I suggest you identify the star performers, namely the authors and facilitators. Trained authors do not necessarily make good facilitators, and you must not expect one person to do both.

- Make adequate time in your schedule to train and bed-in your process mappers before the live workshops start.

- A constant need we have is to maintain senior management buy-in across the business, since this is not a 'one-time' priority. The benefits come from persistent application and we have put in place an ongoing communications plan to maintain awareness and commitment.

What do you expect the IOM to deliver after the project?

The key user impact is the 'My Processes' portal, which is a personal, role-based view of the business processes, relevant documents and key measures. People should be able to use this as a front-end to link from processes to Siebel and SAP at transaction level. That will drastically improve ongoing adoption of new systems and the resultant processes. It will save on a lot of admin and eliminates the need for additional job aids and work instructions. With this in place we have globally auditable processes and a controlled system that is a major contributor to ongoing Change Management. This extends to a transparent environment for supply-chain end-to-end improvements. For example, working with a key supplier who has also adopted the same approach.

Can you summarise the benefits you have obtained so far?

The largest medium- to long-term benefits are that, for the first time, we have a roadmap for getting the right processes in place within the integrated SAP/Siebel implementation.

The IOM has significantly contributed to a rapid implementation. This will have a $1m+ impact in itself. Running global workshops online through the web has provided major time and travel savings as well as savings in testing, deployment of new process, training and quality management. These benefits will multiply as upgrades are deployed.

What challenges lie ahead?

We need to maintain the momentum and consistent approach, despite the time pressure, and manage the roll-out through the multiple releases. Key to this is the work we are doing with the SI to capitalise on potential benefits outside the scope of initial implementation. We must make sure we maintain integrity of the IOM through the ongoing change during the SAP/Siebel deployment phases so that our 360-degree view of systems and processes is maintained. We then need to drive the training through process focus and maintain organisational focus throughout the next 12 months and into the continuous business improvement and process management phases beyond. The benefits do speak for themselves, but can get buried by other agendas, so maintaining their visibility is a key part of what we need to do. This process is not about doing a SAP/Siebel implementation. It's about building a sustainable process/system view that will last beyond implementation, well after the implementers have ridden off into the sunset. It will be our bedrock for the future.

ROI multiplier

Once the IOM is in place it can be used on subsequent or parallel initiatives. What it really does is improve the ROI on these initiatives – or at least give them the chance of delivering on the benefits in their business cases, thereby multiplying your Return on Investment.

The ROI multiplies primarily because the IOM provides a solid starting point. When new initiatives start they normally find that any information on processes, if it exists at all, is out of date and you have to start (yet again) with a clean sheet.[1] Not if you have the IOM with processes already defined. The infrastructure is in place; an access mechanism exists; a common language has been agreed. Since the IOM is already in use, it is up to date and business processes have already been captured and have delivered benefits – the IOM has been adopted and has its supporters within the company. Which in turn drives greater momentum.

Some of the business benefits achieved by clients are impressive, especially when they were establishing the IOM for the first time:

- Assuring compliance with governance, legislation and regulations.
  - 'It provides demonstrable corporate governance, improving business performance and pinpointing shortcomings costing more than £18m.'
    UK construction company

- Reducing software implementation times substantially.
  - 'We successfully implemented SAP in four months.'
    Dutch utility organisation

[1] Re-engineering fatigue sets in. Oh no, not another set of analysts coming to see what we do...

- Improving efficiency and effectiveness, through a focus on 'doing the right things'.
  - We achieved an 80% reduction in textual documents and better focus of activities with the added bonus of a 50% reduction in time spent training new recruits.' *Large medical equipment manufacturer*

- Quickly and proactively responding to new business opportunities, by adopting new initiatives and business models.
  - 'Inefficient textual procedures have been replaced with visual processes which played a significant part in winning more than $30 million of new business in 2003.' *Multinational defence contractor*

- Able to take action quickly if the desired results are not being achieved.
  - 'Company X achieved more after six months than Company Y (parent of Company X) had managed after two years.' *The merger of two telecommunication companies in the US and Holland*

- Continuously improving performance, by refining how they operate.

  - 'This has been an integral process tool which has resulted in actual savings in 2003 of £5.7 million and projected savings of £4.5 million per annum.' *Multinational defence contractor*

Summary of Part II

So that strategic initiatives are adopted consistently you need a shared language which is understood both up and down the organisation, from the CEO to the call centre operator, and across the organisational silos from IT to Finance.

The common language needs to describe changes in activities and behaviour; this is potentially the most complex information to convey and is best described in pictures.

The central source for this information is an Intelligent Operations Manual (IOM):

- because everyone can see it, understand it and use it.

- because it describes the operation of the organisation (People, Process and Performance).

- because it is used to support the operation of the business, and is referenced and changed by the initiatives around the organisation.

By using it you can:

- Define each individual's role, responsibility and accountability.

- Measure and gain visibility of end-to-end process, throughout the organisation.

- Proactively audit conformance to company and regulatory requirements.

- Actively promote collaboration between departments, functions and individuals.

The organisation's initiatives will require transformational change and adoption, which the IOM enables you to deliver more effectively and more transparently. While the results required are measured or described in terms of financial or performance metrics, they are delivered by a change in execution of activities.

The principles are not new, but until now they haven't been achievable. Now there is the existing infrastructure of PCs and servers, ubiquitous communications provided by the internet and affordable software to develop and manage the IOM.

The question is, how can this be applied alongside the existing initiatives that the company is committed to?

Part III takes a look at five typical initiatives, although I could have chosen from a raft of others. I have selected four of these as they seem to be most common in all organisations, and in addition I examine the problem of rapid growth.

PART III: So other people have done it,
but can we?

So far, I have outlined a new approach for getting better results supported by an Intelligent Operations Manual which drives greater adoption for initiatives. This is all about driving results from your current initiatives, not starting more.

The question running through your mind is inevitably whether this is relevant or achievable, based on the multiplicity of initiatives currently running in your company.

What is interesting is that the development of an IOM is a key part of every initiative – even though it may not be called that in your organisation.[1] This approach can be applied to those initiatives that are running in your company. In terms of timing, the earlier it can be implemented in the initiative the better. It can then be reused throughout the initiative. But even at the roll-out stage when the training materials are being created, the IOM is a critical element of training and therefore you can still get value.

Once the IOM is in place it can be reused for all subsequent initiatives and it will put them all into context and ensure that there is consistency on the delivery of the results.

Typical areas where it can be used:

- risk management; identifying operational risk so that business controls can be put in place and managed in the context of the business.

- business continuity management; identifying key points of business risk in the context of the operational processes so that they can be proactively mitigated.

- performance management; driving improved performance through a co-ordinated approach for process and metrics.

- compliance; meeting FDA, Sarbanes-Oxley, Basel II[2] and FSA regulations.

---

[1] Unisys has just started calling it '3D Visible Enterprise'.
[2] Shorthand for 'The Basel II Framework' – regulations that cover capital requirements for banking organisations.

- Merger & Acquisition; due diligence from an operational perspective and delivering the benefits from the transaction.

- software implementation; successful implementation of packaged software (ERP, CRM, SCM, etc) or bespoke/customer-written software.

- Corporate Performance Management; driving improved performance by linking process and metrics, rather than a purely financial planning approach.

- new business launch or opening new operations; developing repeatable blueprints to reduce the time and cost to get up to speed.

- rapid organic growth; coping with stellar expansion and the pressures put on the workforce.

- Six Sigma; a complementary approach which supports this process improvement methodology.

- Total Quality Management; a holistic approach to quality and ISO 9000 compliance.

- Business Process Reengineering; making the changes analysing and improving processes sustainable.

- Business Process Outsourcing (BPO) and Shared Services; managing the interface better, driving increased profitability for the outsourcer, and getting a seamless and cost-effective service for the client.

Chapter 11

To sign or not to sign? – The spectre of compliance

'The biggest challenge is making sure that the bias toward controllership, and the responsibility for effective governance, become part of the fabric of the company. Because quite honestly, none of this is worth doing if five years from now these standards aren't embedded in our operations.'

Eric M. Pillmore, Senior Vice President of Corporate Governance, Tyco

Regulators mean business

In most companies – even the best ones, the annual visit from the regulators was basically seen as the equivalent of a visit from the Grim Reaper. Regulation was just one of those annoying business things that happened. It was a bit like rehearsing for an opening night performance. You knew the date in advance. People rehearsed their roles, worked on their lines and, most importantly, tidied up the paperwork so that everything seemed flawless on inspection day. This is the 'tick in the box' mentality, which makes compliance an overhead cost and something to be minimised. Today, regulation is on the increase and the question has gained more urgency. Clearly, the past solution of 'sweeping the dirt under the rug' is no longer an efficient – not to mention wise – decision.

Today, the Grim Regulator has changed his rules. Showing up on the spot, unannounced, is legitimate and there is also a plethora of new 'rules and regulations' resulting from Sarbanes-Oxley and other such rulings. This area is a brand-new world for many CEOs, regardless of age: it forces you to sign on the dotted line. Your signature says that the figures or business practices are correct. If something turns out to be incorrect, well, to put it simply – it is your fault. Most new regulations place direct responsibility on the person behind the signature. We are back to the days of 'the figures don't lie'. Whoever did the signing better explain why and, while you're at it, a quick call to your lawyer might not be a bad idea!

Companies are now spending millions getting auditors to crawl through their businesses to ensure that the figures being reported are correct. The budget for this is approved easily because it is protecting the CEO and CFO from prison sentences[1] – and they are the people who are signing off the budgets. However, it does not help the companies improve their performance and bottom line. Remember – this audit visit is now an annual (or even quarterly) event that is making the audit firms very wealthy. A better use of that money would be to get everyone to understand and follow the processes so that compliance becomes a natural part of what people do – putting it on the other side of the balance sheet as an asset, not a liability. Something that the auditors would understand, but probably not appreciate. The return to business ethics is upon us. And rightfully so, considering the price that is paid if the company and its CEO and board are found guilty.

 Multiple Choice: How healthy is your company? After the next compliance visit, what are you expecting?

- *A clean bill of health*
- *A slap on the wrist*
- *A fine*
- *A plant to be shut down*
- *A prison sentence.*

See what your CFO, your Compliance Officer, and Accounts Receivable clerk[2] have to say and compare their answers. This will give you a good idea of just how much corporate governance work you have to do.

[1] In the US there are serious prison sentences for white-collar crime, way beyond the traditional one to two years.

[2] Never forget that this person is one of the few who are likely to know which purchase orders will ever be paid, and should therefore be accrued as revenue.

Don't get me wrong. Regulation has a positive side as well – especially in the messy politics of some boardrooms. A client, who works in exclusive high-level investment banking circles, told me that he found the atmosphere of new regulation actually rather useful. Now, rather than spending hours and hours lobbying and chewing people's ears off, all you have to do to get approval for a pet project in board meetings is to say 'This will get us in-line with the international Basel II requirements.'

As colourful as this story might be, what you should be thinking of right now – especially if your title contains CEO, CFO, Corporate Governance, Compliance Officer, President, Vice President or anything remotely resembling compliance responsibility – are some rather critical questions to establish whether the compliance programme is adding any value to the business.

- Put the proof on the table: show me the clause in the regulation.

- What specifically needs to be done?

- Is there anything we need to stop doing? Will this damage the business?

- Is there another solution possible or already in place?

Chicken Little: Regulation is not the end of the world

For those of you who have small children, or can remember the story of Chicken Little, regulation is like the acorn that fell on Chicken Little's head – The sky is falling. The sky is falling.

Nothing could be further from the truth. The most recent PricewaterhouseCoopers Annual CEO Survey (which collects the opinions of nearly 1400 US CEOs) found that 59% saw over-regulation as a very substantial or significant threat to business. That leaves an impressive 41% saying that regulation is a relatively minor or no threat at all. I'm sorry, but 41% sounds like a rather strong minority, so the 59% of you who are looking for an excuse should stop whining about regulation. It isn't the end of the world.[3]

Not the regulation, but response to regulation that matters

Remember a childhood sports coach paraphrasing the American sportswriter Grantland Rice, 'It doesn't matter whether you win or lose, it's how you play the game.' Well, handling regulation is a little bit like this. It is not winning that matters, but how you and your Board react to the rules and regulations in the long run. For some companies, it might be tough at first. It might mean a lot of changes rather quickly. It might mean some pain and agony, but you, your Board and your organisation are going to have to bite the bullet and get on with it. Your choice is to do it well, or do it poorly and call it 'bad luck', 'fate' or 'bad government'. The smart way would be to look the regulations right in the eye and figure out how to work them into your strategy and not re-build your business around the regulation.

An example

Process Management in the medical industry

A merger of two medical device companies required a smooth marriage of the two organisations' established methods of working. The project sought to take the best from each company's best practice and procedure for the future. It was imperative that they gained ISO registration for the merged organisation.

The compliance team realised they could use this as a catalyst for change, to contribute as part of the business, rather than be seen as a necessary evil. In a series of live workshops the staff produced simple, flexible graphical maps to define how the combined business would work. Relevant, existing and new

[3]People constantly say to me 'this is the end of the world' or 'that is the end of the world'. It is not. The end of the world is when it all stops and everything goes black. Point. Everything else can be resolved.

supporting documentation was then linked to the process maps to form a complete model of the business (the IOM). The model was audited by one of the leading Certification bodies in the UK and the company obtained ISO 9000 registration within six months – crucial in this demanding and competitive market.

The benefits of this approach were an 80% reduction in textual documents and better focus of activities. There was greater consistency in working practices and customer service. Training time for new recruits was reduced by 50%, and morale increased across the firm. Three years later, the paper handbooks don't exist because the IOM is used and maintained daily.

As a result of putting the IOM in place, it was available for a new ERP application, so this is an example of leveraging the IOM. The requirements were specified more accurately, which resulted in a better choice of software, and the implementation of the system proved to be quicker and easier than expected.

Chapter 12

Implementing enterprise software applications

'There is about as much evidence for the existence of web services as there is for sex with aliens.'

Robin Bloor of Bloor Research

Enterprise software and its vendors

Software is now critical to virtually every business. It only takes one power outage to realise exactly how much of our equipment has embedded software and runs off a 13-amp mains plug; PCs, phones, photocopiers, networks. Businesses seem to grind to a halt when the network or internet connection goes down. We have now built ourselves a very complex IT infrastructure.

On top of this infrastructure are the 'enterprise applications' which run the day-to-day operations. They cover accounting, procurement, stock control, customer management, etc. These applications access the vast databases which are the heart of our businesses. So dependent are we on these applications that software vendors would have us believe that picking the correct supplier will give us competitive advantage.

The market is dominated in this area by just a two players. The players with revenue greater than $1billion are SAP and Oracle (which is better known for its database). The CRM (Customer Relationship Management) boom, which started in the late 1990s, allowed Siebel to build a serious business, and get bought by Oracle.

Nucleus Research interviews clients of software vendors (whom the software vendors themselves have named as references) to understand what, if any, Return on Investment (ROI) they received. Nucleus really made their name after the Siebel study was published, which reported that 61% of their reference customers failed to get a positive ROI, and that the average cost per user was $18,000. I don't expect Nucleus Research are on Tom Siebel's Christmas card list.

The purpose of my telling you this is not to beat up Siebel, (sadly, most other software vendors do not do well either) but to illustrate that the effective implementation of enterprise software is critical to the business. Poorly implemented, it can cost an enormous amount – or it could even kill your business.

The history of massive failures, or at least no ROI, is long and well publicised – and a number of well-known clients appear throughout the lists. I estimate that 70% of all major projects over $100m NEVER EVEN FINISH – let alone deliver benefits. These failing projects even have a name... 'runaways'.[1]

A few examples from a very long list:

- Fox-Meyer Corp. A bungled ERP implementation forced the drug distributor into bankruptcy, and they raised a claim for $1bn in damages against SAP AG, SAP America Inc and Andersen Consulting.

- Hershey spent $112m with IBM to roll out SAP, Siebel and Manugistics, causing a 12% ($100m) drop in sales in the quarter after going live. Software and business-process fixes took over a year.

- A UK survey of Government IT projects totalling £10bn in value found that only 13% were successful (on time, to specification, to cost).[2]

But why do companies embark on software implementation programmes that cost millions and could bankrupt the company? The reasons for taking the risks include:

[1] I spent five years taming those runaways. In most cases they could be saved and delivered. But on a couple of occasions the only thing to do was get out the humane killer and put them out of their misery – before any more money was wasted.

[2] This does not even consider adoption. What would the result be if this were included as a measure of success – 1%, 2%?

- integration/maintenance costs of the existing systems are becoming unacceptable

- the current systems are preventing growth or changes to working practices

- a recent merger or acquisition has left the company with incompatible systems

- IT staff want SAP/Oracle/Siebel on their CV (seriously...).

But no matter which software vendor you choose, or how good their application, a major risk is still the integration with your existing applications. Now the IT people will talk excitedly about how web-services will allow them to easily link different applications and how the interfaces will be trivial. More like Trivial Pursuit – popular bar-talk, requires answers to obscure questions, nobody really feels like they've won and takes longer than you thought when you first started.[3]

On a brighter note...

But is there a better way, that has been proven for client after client? In my experience there is. But it does require a different approach and way of thinking. And it is proven across the world.

The different process-focused approach I've explained has such staggering results that many of the consultants and system integrators I work alongside almost refuse to believe it is true.

The result is faster (hence cheaper and higher ROI), lower risk, and better ROI due to more complete business transformation. Pie in the sky? Not for a number of companies. Limited to single location? Not at all. Limited to one sort of enterprise application? Certainly not.

[3]Yes, I'm a poor loser at Trivial Pursuit.

So how is this approach different?

In summary, the approach is to take a process and performance focus to the implementation. Work out, in operational terms, what the business is trying to achieve. Document this and manage it in the IOM. The tools currently used are still stuck in the 1970s – normally it is MSOffice.[4] There are now tools designed specifically for the task, but they are not yet widely known about – hence people still use MSOffice or a diagramming tool.

 Ask your business analyst to show you a copy of the processes that are being used to specify your enterprise application. Is it a hierarchy, a 45-foot long piece printout covered in processes, a 50-page MSWord document, or a wall covered in post-it notes? Then ask yourself, 'Who needs to see and use it every day?'

There is now a stronger emphasis on limiting programming changes to the enterprise software (keeping it vanilla) and changing the company's business processes. This makes the IOM an even more critical part of the implementation, as the project is focused on business transformation and training. No longer is it just the repository for the software configuration documentation.

Looking at a typical six-stage implementation cycle, let's contrast the old approach, with an approach leveraging the power of the IOM.

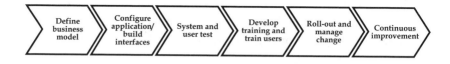

Define business model | Configure application/ build interfaces | System and user test | Develop training and train users | Roll-out and manage change | Continuous improvement

[4]Staggering that the enterprise applications have improved massively, but the tools (MSOffice) are the ones I was using ten years ago.

1. Define business model (requirements capture)

Before: Flipcharts, MSWord and MSPowerpoint used to define transformational change.
With IOM: Capture end-to-end processes in live workshops; drill down to more detail; attach documentation and applications; link to requirements database; show phased releases as scenarios; perform impact analysis at process level; apply version control; perform business process comparison/analysis; and create database and repository of business processes. This is all held and managed in the IOM.
Benefits: Agreement/consensus reached more quickly. Integrity maintained between process levels. 'Quick win' projects identified. Effective Release and Scope Management from process perspective. Improved communication and knowledge transfer through creation of a central information repository. Therefore: **reduced cost, accelerated implementation, reduced risk, improved delivery**.

2. Configure application and build interfaces

Before: Application configured from MSWord specifications.
With IOM: IOM used to configure application. Model revised as requirements change. Interface design specifications attached to process model.
Benefits: Less ambiguity so more accurate configuration. Business model reflects the current thinking. Interfaces designed from process perspective. Issues fed back to process owners. Therefore: **reduced cost, improved accuracy**.

3. System and user test

Before: Test scripts written and tests performed against them.
With IOM: Business model used as basis of tests, so up to date. Tests from end-to-end process perspective, so proves entire operation, not just specific systems or interfaces.
Benefits: Entire business operation proved. More consistent, complete and relevant testing. Tests performed more quickly. No test scripts need to be created. Therefore: **reduced cost, reduced risk**.

4. Develop training and train users

Before: Training material and user procedures based on new software functionality.

With IOM: Users trained using the live web-based IOM, which defines new business operation and has links to supporting software screen/transactions, forms, documentation and self-help. This supports the business transformation/change management.

Benefits: Training targeted at business transformation, not software functionality. No training or user procedure development. Reduced training requirement as model is intuitive and complete. Focused new employee orientation. Therefore: **cost reduced, business transformation delivered, ROI accelerated**

5. Roll-out and change management

Before: Training on software considered sufficient, and change management often ignored.

With IOM: IOM can determine change in working practices and scale of change management task. As the IOM is delivered through a web-based process portal it can be used as self-help, showing activities and links to all supporting documentation activities required to perform a task.

Benefits: Change Management recognised as discipline. Business Model reduces risk and effort of Change Management. Therefore: **ROI accelerated, reduced cost, reduced risk**

6. Continuous improvement

Before: What?

With IOM: IOM managed within the process portal which has collaborative functionality aimed at promoting a culture of measurable, continuous improvement – by users.

Benefits: Benefits continue after project complete. Ensured compliance and quality through collaborative use and documentation of standards. Therefore: **improved profitability, reduced cost, increased ROI.**

It sounds so good – why isn't everyone on this page?

So if this approach can dramatically change the results of an implementation of a major enterprise application – why isn't everyone doing it? There are two reasons:

- the approach is not (yet) widely publicised so you and System Integrators are not likely to have encountered it. Also, at first glance this approach is not dissimilar to what they are currently doing.[6]

- most enterprise applications are managed by large System Integrators who are normally contracted to implement the software, *not help you transform the business*. There is little incentive for them to try a different approach as they perceive 'different = risk' and 'risk = cost'. So they fall back on their trusted MSWord templates for capturing requirements and configuring software.[7]

What needs to change? You need to consider the overall transformation of the business as the primary aim of the project, and the installation of the software as secondary. This will change how you incentivise and engage the Systems Integrators. The changes can be summarised as:

- Business transformation not software configuration

- End user engagement not software installation

- Paid by adoption, not fixed price or time and materials.

These changes in approach can be (and are being) used with the traditional large-scale implementations of SAP, Oracle and Siebel, and smaller implementations of other applications. Let me end this chapter with a success story.

---

[6]If you leave the UK and steer just 5 degrees off course, you don't hit the Bahamas, but hit South America instead. Small change, big effect.
[7]Not quite the 'thought leadership' their marketing expounds.

An example

International J. D. Edwards implementation

A multinational company employing 4,000 people in 39 countries has been at the forefront of its industry for over 100 years. They manufacture process fluid control products that are used in all forms of industry from chemical plants and refineries to hospital heating systems.

Following the appointment of a new CEO, cross-company integration was introduced as an objective to improve the way information was shared on a global basis. They wanted to put in place an IOM that could be shared and tailored for local differences.

Central to this strategy was the standardisation of back-office systems and a drive towards using IT more effectively to bring about efficiency improvements within the business.

Like many multinational companies, each country used local IT solutions, many of which needed replacing or updating to meet the challenges of global trading and also to achieve Euro compliance. The lack of a centrally co-ordinated approach meant higher costs across the company, inconsistency in reporting, and, ultimately, impact on the customer experience.

This situation was compounded by the fact that each country had its own business processes and documentation, making standardisation difficult at best, with a high-risk factor for the successful implementation of business changes.

They recognised the inefficiency of this approach but didn't have a formal methodology for documenting and comparing internal business processes from country to country. They did, however, believe that a 'common process thread' could be found throughout the group, given the transparency and visibility through the IOM.

They set out in Spain to replace their ERP system. Prior to putting the IOM in place they implemented J. D. Edwards' 'One World' software in France and the UK. It made sense to take the

French implementation and use this as a basis for Spain. This meant taking the French business processes and applying them to Spain so that 'One World' could be implemented. It soon became clear that the processes from the French implementation were not designed to be reused and that it would be almost impossible to replicate the 'One World' system in the other countries.

By developing the IOM for the Spanish implementation they were able to provide a foundation for managing the 'change process' that the company was about to undergo – a situation they recognised to be fraught with risk. Despite initial resistance to this approach by the Spanish, the benefits of using the IOM quickly became clear, both for delivering short-term process and communication improvements as well as clearing the way for a smooth implementation of their ERP system.

The processes were captured and documented over a three month pre-implementation phase, highlighting areas for improvement within existing processes. But more importantly this allowed people to clearly see the need and implications of making those changes, i.e. adoption was built into the earliest phases of the project.

Another benefit was derived as they were able to identify the connections between different areas of the business, so the training focused on the processes rather than the ERP software functionality. This was particularly important in a Spanish business culture with little experience of the concept of ERP software.

The ERP software was implemented in Spain in six months with 'buy-in' from users at all levels and this also included the development of the IOM. The implementation was significantly more successful than the UK or French implementations: faster, smoother and better adoption.

This very positive experience of the Spanish implementation is being used to develop a blueprint for subsequent rollouts of

ERP implementations. The high-level process maps will allow the management within other countries to, at the very least, review their own processes and see how closely they align to the model in Spain.

'This approach helped us to manage the ERP implementation in a much more "controlled" way and also provided us with blueprint documentation for subsequent roll-outs,' says the Group Systems Manager. 'Spain was the smoothest ERP implementation I have ever experienced within our company.'

Chapter 13

We've outsourced – that means this is not my problem, right?

'If you don't know enough to run it, you don't know enough to outsource it.'

Ian Gotts

Is this relevant to me?

For outsourcing read 'Business Process Outsourcing (BPO) or Shared Service Centres'.[1] This chapter describes what an organisation should consider when outsourcing a business unit. It is relevant to companies implementing the internal version of outsourcing: transferring responsibility to an internal shared service centre. This is sometimes seen as a prelude to outsourcing, but it needn't be.

While the discussion around people and processes in this chapter does not seem directly relevant to IT outsourcing where the focus is on a third-party operating data centres or desktop machines, it is relevant to the 'people' side of that operation; the working practices surrounding how the datacentre is run, how an upgrade to the desktop is managed, etc.

The increase in outsourcing

We outsource some of our development work and inbound calls at my company – and I'm pretty sure you have too – or at least considered it. Despite controversy around outsourcing, especially of the offshore kind, it is growing rapidly. Gartner estimates that worldwide business process outsourcing revenues will grow to $173.1bn in 2007.

[1] Using this shorthand will make this chapter easier to read, and about a page shorter.

In the US and UK recently there has been an uproar about companies outsourcing their call centres to India. Some companies have brought them back in-house for valuable client groups. But the economics are compelling, enabled by cheap telecoms. India has a huge supply of graduate-level staff who are keen, enthusiastic and a fraction (less than 20%) of the cost of their US or UK counterparts. Think of the dramatic impact that this will have on the local economy in India over the next ten years.

Not only is the number of organisations that outsource increasing, but also the scope of what can be, and has been, outsourced successfully. While procurement or HR are natural candidates, virtually any business process can be outsourced. I know of one oil company that operates as a virtual company by outsourcing practically every area of its business – so, in essence, it works as a 'prime contractor'.

Why outsource?

What this has made people consider is – 'What are our core competencies that add value to our company's objectives?' There is a strong and reasonable case for only outsourcing activities that are non-core.[2] But what is core? Is it the call centre that is dealing with all our customer interactions? Is it the delivery of our product? The development of new product?[3]

Many outsourcing arrangements are tactical and tied to cost-cutting. While outsourcing is often carried out to reduce cost, it is also done to access multi-skilled staff, to improve flexibility and to gain economies of scale.

Accenture, in one of its recent multinational surveys, found that a full 86% of executives realised control gains over business results – most within the first year of outsourcing. These control gains include:

- Better planning capabilities
- More reliable business information

[2]So if people are a company's greatest asset, why is HR the first part of the organisation to be outsourced... when they control the quality and development of the people? Pret à Manger, the sandwich chain, calls recruitment 'Treasure Hunting'. [3]Much of pharmaceutical R&D is outsourced by buying companies that are developing promising drugs.

- Reduced spending levels
- Improved variability of costs
- Stronger grasp of business outcomes

Collectively, these control increases enable organisations to achieve high performance on two fronts. They help to deliver current earnings. And they lay the groundwork for future growth – across business cycles and industry disruptions.

An example

Revenues of £220m, profits of £60m, 24 staff (yes – 24). Now I know the CFOs out there will have their calculators ready and be working out the profitability of their own organisation if it were based on this business model.

It is a real company – an oil company operating predominantly in the North Sea. Their expertise is in acquiring interests in plots of seabed – called blocks – to explore, develop and produce. A few years ago, they acquired an interest in some blocks later found to contain one of the largest oil reserves discovered in the North Sea in recent years. They focus their core skills on what can deliver the highest value improvement to their company (finding, drilling, producing and selling oil and gas). They do this as a non-operating partner, managing their interests in blocks to outsourced operators and subcontractors for everything from exploration to field abandonment.

They know the industry and are consummate outsourcers. Put another way, they understand their core skills, they understand exactly what it takes to do all the jobs that have been outsourced. They know them so well, that they are able to define the correct metrics (SLA) to manage and drive the subcontractors. They primarily focus on where and how to use their core skills to extract added value for their stakeholders.

 Subcontractors (outsourcers) focus on the delivery of their SLAs with laser precision – nothing else.

For example, for every barrel of oil you extract from a field you need to pump in a number of barrels of water to stop the field reservoir pressure from decreasing, and thereby reducing its production capacity. For every barrel of water injected back into the field you get additional oil out. Therefore it is as critical that the water injection plant is operational 24/7 as it is for the oil production plant. Unless water injection is an SLA, then the subcontractor is unlikely to invest in keeping the water injection plant at this level of availability.

The successful oil business I am describing put in place an IOM long before we knew what it was called. They called it the 'Coalface to Stakeholder Interface'. This is their business mapped out in process terms, both internally and externally, with metrics and supporting documents linked in the correct context. It links the drivers of the stakeholders with the actions of the coalface. It makes the delivery of success and failure transparent to all parties involved. This is used by the internal team and subcontractors to manage performance to budgets, and stretch targets.

The Engineering and Production Director commented, 'I was looking for a tool that would glue everything together so we could create a focus for the business and enable it to move forward quickly. We had a long list of capabilities and functionality we wanted. I'd tried to put it in place at a US oil service company where I worked some ten years earlier but, at the time, the functionality and infrastructure were not available and the bespoke software costs were prohibitive.'

How to get the correct Service Level Agreement (SLA)

The moment the ink is signed on the contract with the outsourcer your fate is sealed.[4]

Think of the outsource organisation not as a third party but as another department of your own company. Of course it isn't so cosy, but the interfaces are still there and are critical. There needs to be a seamless delivery between your business

[4]We should never forget this statement. That is why I have underlined it.

and theirs. This is particularly true if they are handling front-line interaction with your customers.

Unfortunately most outsourcing deals end up focusing on the Service Level Agreement (SLA). These are the numbers by which the outsourcer will be judged and normally paid. But if you don't know in detail how your business operates and what is outsourced, then how can you agree the correct SLAs?

By 'What' I mean:

- what scope
- what cost
- what performance
- what people ...[5]

Clear definition of the above will determine the correct SLA, and, whatever SLAs are agreed, this is what the outsourced company will deliver. Nothing else. Nothing more.

 If you ask anyone to do something that you do not fully understand – expect to pay through the nose.

Think back to the oil company example. If water injection uptime wasn't an SLA then the outsourcer would not have the budget (or incentive) to deliver on it – with disastrous effect.

You can also expect to pay heavily for any change in scope, SLA, etc. Often the outsourcer has had to offer a price to win the work that is lower than his operating cost, but expects to make up the shortfall in change requests – high priced changes to the service you are locked into.

Interestingly, if you do the (process) work to really understand what you are outsourcing, and then put in place the key metrics, you may find you have achieved the savings you were looking for in the outsourced contract... but

[5]Strictly 'which people', not what, but then the sentence doesn't really work. If you want a book on punctuation read: *Eats, Shoots & Leaves* by Lynne Truss. She goes for a zero tolerance approach to grammatical lapses. It's a bestseller in its own right!

without the contract negotiation, TUPE of staff,[6] risk of transfer of work to an outsourcing vendor, ongoing management of the relationship, etc.

When not to outsource

You are not ready to outsource if any of the following apply:

- you can't manage the area, or don't have skilled managers
- the costs are out of control
- you don't understand whether it is performing
- you don't know how to improve its performance
- you aren't confident about the current metrics/measurements.

Outsourcers are commercial businesses. They are growing rapidly and are becoming accustomed to healthy profits. Therefore they are looking to:

- increase profits (picking clients who are basket cases, weak players, or who don't understand their costs)
- maximise lock-in (positioning themselves to extend the contract)
- make money out of change requests (exploiting a client's lack of understanding of their own needs).

 Take a look at your recent outsourcing or Shared Service Centre initiative in this context.

Outsourcing and the IOM

There is a valuable role for the IOM where it can dramatically improve the level of service you can get from your outsourcer. Remember the IOM can give an end-to-end process view of the business. It helps processes cross the organisational boundaries or silos. Those boundaries are simply better defined and managed than in an SLA or outsource contract.

It doesn't matter whether you are: thinking of outsourcing;

[6]UK: The Transfer of Undertakings (Protection of Employment) Regulations 1981 – commonly known as the TUPE Regulations – safeguard employees' rights where businesses change hands between employers.

have just signed a contract; are midway through a seven-year contract; or are insourcing – bringing the work back in-house.

I want to look at each of these situations…

1. You are considering outsourcing

This is the perfect time to put the IOM in place – while you are still uncommitted. The IOM will allow you to clearly scope what area of the business you are outsourcing.[7] If you define in the IOM the area you are considering outsourcing and its related processes, you will get a clear understanding of the complete processes and where the interfaces to the outsourced areas are. By listing the resources associated with each activity you will quickly see which staff will go or need to be redeployed due to the outsourcing, and their costs. In addition, you will also see where you are losing a role or individual who is used elsewhere in the business.

Once the processes are agreed in the IOM, then you have the ability to work out what measurements or metrics really drive them. These are the metrics that should go to make up the SLAs. This is the most critical part of the work – but is worthless unless the processes really reflect what happens in the business.

So, by now you will have identified:

- scope: which processes
- resources: which people
- metrics: what SLA.

You can also apply Activity Based Costing (ABC) to the IOM. By this I mean that average durations can be assigned to each activity, to which the volumes flowing through each activity can be added. Once you have worked out the loaded resource rates you can calculate (or the IOM can for you) the total cost of running the operation. Now you can see what it really costs you to run the area, and therefore whether it is worth outsourcing.

[7]Interestingly, one of the major outsourcing companies uses this approach with an 'HR blueprint IOM' and takes clients through it in a live workshop to scope the work.

As an example, this will show you that the area costs £30m per year to run, so the quote from the outsourcer of £45m per year is outrageous. Bearing in mind that once you've outsourced the area you no longer have the data to perform the ABC modelling, it is difficult to renegotiate from a position of strength mid-contract. Therefore the work to create the IOM saved you being overcharged £15m per year, and let's assume a five-year contract...

.... that is a total saving of £75m.

Without the IOM you are entering into the negotiation with the outsourcer blind. They have (probably) done it a number of times and have a reasonable view of the cost to deliver the service. The less of a grasp you have on the true operational cost, the more profit there is in the contract for them.[8]

Using the IOM, you can transition the work to the outsourcer more easily. This is 'big risk' time, especially if the work is going offshore. You want (and your customers demand) continuity of service through this period of major change and upheaval.

Here's a thought – build the IOM with the outsourcer, have your (remaining) IT department host it for them so that you still have access to it, and then you can see the continuous improvement that they are putting in. Then they don't hold all the cards when it is time to renegotiate the contract.

For example, the UK Government's (Inland Revenue) IT outsourcing supplier was (until 2004) EDS. At the outset of the bidding process for the renewal of the contract it was rumoured that they had such a strong position after their ten-year contract that no-one wanted to bid when the contract came up for renewal. The Government had to explicitly encourage a number of suitable vendors to bid and therefore generate competition.

Even better than just hosting the IOM – mandate the principle of the IOM on the outsourcer in the contract, and then ensure it is kept up to date and returned at the end of the contract.

---

[8]A number of outsourcing firms have recognised that if their clients develop the IOM before they sign the contract, then they understand their costs and a lot of the profit disappears – so they'd prefer it if the IOM was the outsourcer's tool.

2. You've just signed the contract

If you happen to be in the process of transitioning work to the outsourcer then it is not too late. However, there is going to be a fair amount of resistance from the outsourcer as they are committed to deliver a service by a certain date and they will brush aside anything they perceive as a delay or increased risk.

You should focus on the interfaces between yourself and the outsourcer in the IOM. You are unlikely to have time to go back and define the processes in detail. But if you have, re-read the previous section.

If you have the time and resources to be able to get the interface processes in the IOM, then the focus of the effort should be on your internal processes up to where they touch the outsourcer. To understand the validity of the SLAs you've signed you should define the processes that you've outsourced, at a high level. If you can work with the outsourcer – brilliant.

When you have this information in the IOM you can determine the correct SLAs and the right values for them. Don't be surprised if the outsourcer isn't very happy – or alternatively if they get very excited and want to take the IOM from you.

Now may be the right time to renegotiate the SLAs before the whole new outsourcing team is organised around meeting your original SLAs. Bite the bullet and do it. There are potentially millions at stake.

You can use the IOM to manage the relationship between the company and the outsourcer – across the boundary. Boundaries that are vigorously defended once the contract is signed.

Finally, you can use the IOM to judge how the outsourcer is doing in terms of business improvement. If they are delivering the contract for less than you have estimated from your version of the IOM, it may be that they:

- are using offshore staff

- misjudged the cost and therefore will make it back in change requests

- misjudged the cost and will go bust, leaving you in the lurch.

3. If you are in the middle of a seven-year contract

If you are in the middle of a long-term contract, or due to renegotiate, then you need to implement much of the previous section. Picking the right time is important as the desire to do the work and your internal resources may be in limited supply. You may need to wait for a catalyst – major problem with outsourcer performance; breakdown at the interface; re-negotiation due.

If you are in the run-up to the re-tendering of the contract, you may be able to persuade the incumbent outsourcer to help you build the IOM so they can demonstrate how valuable they are, and it will increase their chance of winning the re-tender.

4. Insourcing

Insourcing is the same as launching a whole new business unit. You have a chance to start with a clean sheet – a greenfield site.[9] The IOM will enable you to bring back in-house processes which are 'best-practice' and are tailored for your business. The ability to understand how the outsourcer has been operating will be invaluable when you start to define the processes you are bringing back in-house. It is important to negotiate this with the outsourcer as part of their exit.

The outsourcing relationship

This seems to suggest that the relationship between client and outsourcer can be highly confrontational, and in many cases it is. Badly designed SLAs drive a wedge between the

[9] The reason God made the world in six days – and had the seventh day to rest – was because he had a greenfield site.

client and outsourcer. The client wants a better service, but the SLA motivates the outsourcer to deliver something else.

Having the IOM in place can start to focus the discussion and allow the relationship to be what it really ought to be – a strategic sourcing relationship.

The Financial Director for the London Stock Exchange, which outsourced its IT function, commented, 'The relationship the Exchange has forged with its supplier is based on give and take, underpinned by an incentive structure that motivates both parties to operate in a spirit of true collaboration.'

 What incentive structures have you put in place with your strategic supplier?

Chapter 14

Six Sigma

'In Six Sigma, processes are where the action is.'

Pete Pande, *Author of* Six Sigma Way

The IOM complements Six Sigma

Six Sigma has a very powerful following in the US and is now gathering momentum in Europe. While originally aimed at manufacturing, there is a strong take-up in financial services where blue-collar productivity gains are being replicated in white-collar industries.

Some of you may have had experience of Six Sigma on a discrete project – but it is worth explaining it in terms of a strategic initiative. It is not a product, and it is not a step-by-step methodology. It is a set of principles that is supported by intensive training which leads to the awarding of yellow, green or black belts, depending on the level of proficiency. It is a business improvement approach which focuses on processes and the measurement of those processes to identify improvements.

Perhaps Six Sigma is best known for its aim for perfection – perfection defined as 99.9997% of cases. This is gauged through measurement, whether quantifying customer satisfaction and needs or assessing that production specifications are met, and confirms that these measurements are gained repeatedly at this high level. However, the Six Sigma approach also recognises the need for organisations to take risks in order to strive for perfection, and tolerates failure as part of the risk-taking strategy.

Jack Welch, ex-CEO of General Electric, had tremendous success with Six Sigma and really put it on the map. Operating margins that were stuck at 10% jumped to 15%. At GE Capital they streamlined paperwork, resulting in more quickly completed deals. Six Sigma taught employees about processes so that staff could be moved easily among GE Divisions. GE even tied 40% of manager bonuses to Six Sigma performance.

However, Welch freely admits in his book[1] that critical to the success of the Six Sigma projects were some basic principles – clear leadership, shared language, common approach and investment in training.

Therefore Six Sigma is complemented perfectly by the principle of an IOM and the approaches suggested for developing the IOM. That is why Pete Pande, Six Sigma guru and author of the 'bible' on the subject, recognises that our approach will help direct and co-ordinate discrete Six Sigma projects so that they deliver greater value to the company as a whole.

So where does the IOM fit?

There are three key areas where the IOM supports Six Sigma:

1. Context setting

Six Sigma is focused at the operational level where the activity happens and where the results can be measured, improvements identified and changes made. And it is very good at that.

The IOM puts in place the higher-level structure and context for the Six Sigma initiative. It helps clarify the scope of the initiative and ensures related initiatives do not overlap or conflict. Savings made by one initiative can force the costs into another area – only to find that an initiative started there forces the costs back. The IOM is the repository for the

[1]Called, inventively, *Jack*.

documentation generated by the initiative that drives adoption of the changes generated by the initiative.

This means getting the senior management or divisional management to define the top-level end-to-end processes. These are broken down hierarchically until you get to the level of the Six Sigma initiative. You may find that this will change the scope of the initiative to ensure that it is consistent with the top-level end-to-end processes.

 If you add up all the savings from the Six Sigma initiatives, are they more than the annual revenue of the company? If they are, then you need the IOM.

2. Documentation standard

Six Sigma is an approach. It does not mandate any documentation standards. Each initiative may invent its own standard or the company may impose a corporate one. Regardless, these are likely to be different from any other initiative running in the company.

The IOM combines the processes, metrics and a mechanism for improvement. Interestingly, just as there are no prescribed documentation standards, there are also no tools. Some modelling products have Six Sigma specific versions which have support for Statistical Process Control. While this is useful, it doesn't drive the real benefits that are derived when Six Sigma is implemented holistically throughout the company. That is why Pete Pande endorses our approach[2].

3. Sustaining improvements

A problem that sometimes occurs with Six Sigma, as with many business improvement approaches, is that the benefits are not sustainable. They are supported by highly trained teams rather than having the end users driving the improvements. It is easy for the end users to disassociate themselves from the results, as they feel no ownership for the process models and performance metrics.

Once the team of black belts has left, the process model

[2]Pete Pande, author of *Six Sigma Way* and *Six Sigma Leader*

isn't maintained and the savings slip away as poor working practices creep back in. Because the development of the IOM encourages end-user participation, and as it is the source of information that is accessed regularly and it is easy to maintain, there is more likely to be a sense of ownership by the end users. Therefore it is used to harness and manage ongoing change. This is the most critical part of any business improvement program – getting end users to continue to drive improvements.

An example

GE used Six Sigma to make a good company stronger, but Motorola used it to save a dying company. The approach adopted in Motorola's communication division in 1987 improved product quality from poor to near perfect. Employment levels increased and from 1987 to 1997 there was a five-fold increase in sales revenue, with profits growing by 20%. Motorola credited $14 billion in savings to Six Sigma.

When is the best time to get started?

Individual Six Sigma initiatives are short-focused activities, although the overall use of Six Sigma will be a long-term strategic initiative. Therefore, once the decision to use the IOM to support the Six Sigma improvements has been made, then it can be used from the start of the next initiative.

Prior to embarking on this course, it is extremely useful to define the highest-level end-to-end processes with the management team. This will set the context for all the Six Sigma initiatives as I described a little earlier.

This is the end of the chapter, so why so little on Six Sigma, I hear you ask? I think it is because the Six Sigma approach and the principles of the IOM are so closely aligned. The argument for why and when to use it is very simple. Part IV of this book will show you how to develop the IOM and combine this with how you have decided to implement Six Sigma.

Chapter 15

We're growing so fast, it's like herding cats

CEO, in yearly company meeting:
'For the fourth year running we have exceeded our estimates
for the year. I don't know what to do.'
From the back of the room:
'Fire the estimator!'

Managing explosive growth

I am sure your company has a long-term growth strategy and a short-term growth plan. Mine has. We have defined quarterly milestones we have to achieve. Everyone knows how hard it is. Boards of directors are beating the hell out of CEOs to find a way to grow. Sales teams are pounding the pavement. The federal government is studying ways to fire up the economy. But in the end, there is not a lot of growth happening.

However, even now there are companies who have got that marketing, product, customer bit right at a sweet spot in the market and are experiencing enormous growth. But it is not that easy to handle. I can hear those companies who are struggling to survive saying 'nice problem to have'. But it is a tough one. *Fortune* Magazine has been tracking the global 100 fastest growing companies annually since 2001 and there are few companies that make the list repeatedly. In Deloitte & Touches' Technology FAST 500 Index only one company made it to the list every year since the programme's inception in 1995.

Why are success stories so limited? As paradoxical as it sounds, one of the toughest problems facing many of today's most successful companies is success itself. Recent history abounds with examples of companies whose overnight success led to morning-after failure because their managers lacked the experience needed to manage explosive growth.

What to do when you grow by 500% per year...

The only way to sustain competitive advantage is to ensure that your organisation is learning faster than the competition. There is significant correlation between learning speed and competitiveness as well as between learning speed and innovation. But when growth is explosive and people are continuing to join on a daily basis, what can you do?

The biggest issue with rapid growth is keeping the quality of staff you recruit high, and being able to keep them. As you grow, jobs will become better defined. In the early days you'll need people willing to take on all kinds of tasks, but once you start to expand, you'll need specialists. People make your company tick. Without them, you won't execute the aggressive deadlines that investors expect and which a competitive market requires. Going from employee number one to employee number 50 is one thing. Going from employee 50 to employee 2,000 – provided you get that far – is quite another. Concerns about shortages of qualified workers are increasing in many industries, especially in relation to organisational ability to address the continuing challenge of sustained rapid growth. Part of the reason for your early success is that you were small and focused.

 Excellent people recruit even better people. Average people recruit mediocre people, mediocre people recruit weak people and so on...

What do you need to manage?

It feels like there are a million things which are critical, so you need to focus on the half-dozen that make all the difference. Here are my top six:

1. Consistent message and objectives

New staff arrive with very little understanding of the business and its objectives. They will have formed some opinions through the interview process. Ideally they should spend an hour one-to-one with the CEO or management team to get a real understanding of the company's strategy and direction. Clearly that is not possible when there could be 50 or 200 new recruits per month.

Therefore the top-level diagrams in the IOM set out the operational strategy in terms of activities and metrics. This is reinforced down through each level. The new recruit can put their role into context, and their manager will find it easier to explain the operation of his or her team in relation to the company. The new joiner can go back and revisit these diagrams, once their head has stopped spinning and as they get a feel for the company – rather than try to refer to notes taken when the CEO gave a hasty 30-minute presentation to this month's group of new employees.

2. Central 'source of truth'

Once you've recruited all these people they need to be well directed – or at least have a strong idea of the company strategy, its principles and objectives. You haven't time for lengthy induction courses, and their boss may have been in the role for only a few months.

The IOM is used as the 'self-help operations manual'. It is online, it is current, it is the 'single source of truth'. Forcing everybody to use and access it will drive consistency. But coercion is not the best way. You're growing fast and people who are under pressure will take the easiest route.

Careful thought about making the IOM the easiest place to get the right information will pay dividends. Go to your marketing people to get them to support you in terms of branding. Talk to end users to find out what other information would be useful to store in the IOM. It is something as simple as putting the daily canteen/restaurant menus in an information area. Often non-core processes that are used infrequently tempt people to start using the IOM, such as 'Upgrading your mobile phone' or 'Filling out expenses'. One company branded their IOM 'How2' and the first processes were related to internal IT support – 'How to get your PC fixed'. The name says everything.

One of the most interesting points of the IOM is that it reduces induction time. People spend less time getting up to speed. They don't need to spend weeks and weeks in induction courses learning their job – much of which gets forgotten anyway, as it is not applied immediately. Instead, the training involves showing people how to access and navigate around the IOM and then builds in some specific on-the-job training for their immediate role.

Once we put the IOM in place I've seen the time taken for raw graduates on our support desk to become fully proficient drop from eight weeks to two weeks.

3. Recruitment process

The engine of the business is choosing the right people. Having a clear, consistent, accountable process for recruiting them that is easy to use – i.e. getting from 'Identified resource need' to 'first day in post' – is critical. That process will be used 20, 200 or 2000 times by many different people. This is a key part of the IOM. It is not part of the core end-to-end process such as C2C (Client to Cash), but it is a support process, rather like the 'Deliver IT infrastructure' process. Within the support process there is an end-to-end process. I've often heard the HR processes called R2R – Recruit to Retire.[1]

Don't forget the exit process. Recruiting at this rate means you are bound to get PURE candidates.[2] The exit process, unless it is well documented and can be followed to the letter, burns up more management time than recruitment. That is because of the fear of a claim for unfair dismissal. Alternatively you give away too much as a payment as part of the compromise agreement. Finally, a person leaving is important feedback on the company's performance, which may need to be fed back into the IOM to change the way the company operates.

[1] The second R used to be Retire, but more recently it has stood for Redundancy or Resignation. [2] PURE – Previously Unidentified Recruiting Error.

4. Metrics

At a massive growth rate you need leading not lagging indicators. Cash is an important metric. Many profitable companies have failed because they grew too fast for their cashflow, with the result that they let customers down, or ended up owned by their Venture Capitalists. Spotting a downward trend in revenue or an upward trend in terms of debtor days is clearly critical.

 Never go back to the Venture (Vulture) Capitalists when you really need the money. Go to them when you can afford to walk away if you don't like their terms.

Lagging indicators such as revenue reported monthly or quarterly are of little use. You need early warning indicators. Those high-level metrics will be built of lower-level metrics such as 'average discount being given on orders' which may indicate a drop in profitability, or 'customer churn' which indicates a more serious problem.

Without processes linked to metrics you really are flying blind. But getting leading indicators is not just about providing the lagging metrics more quickly. It is about rethinking, in the context of your processes, what measures will drive the correct behaviour and give you early warning. Every business should do this, but those that are more stable have less of a need. For a rapidly growing business it is essential. Development of the IOM is the way to define the processes and metrics. It is also where they are displayed so everyone in the organisation sees the same picture and is therefore working towards a common aim.

5. Management of change

An organisation of 100 is very different to one of 1000 or 10,000. So as you grow you know that you will go through constant change: changes to organisational structure, roles, processes, objectives, suppliers and alliances. For technology companies the changes are even more dramatic as 'Crossing the Chasm'[3] has shown. Therefore, you should put in place the mechanism to manage the change as early as possible – while there are as few people as possible. The change mechanism is driven around the IOM. Ideally the IOM will have the workflow to support the sign-off and version control, which means that despite the changes the business is still compliant. This audit trail is just as important to the business as the auditors, because the pace of change means that you may need to roll-back to a previous version if you find the changed processes are not working.

6. Getting adoption and buy-in

People are so busy with their day jobs, they are very unlikely to want to devote time to something that seems to be a documentation exercise. You need to lead from the top and appoint a project manager whose skin is as thick as a rhino's, you need to pick the first areas to define that are useful to the individual users, and finally you need to cut off all the other places they can go to for the information.

In my organisation we've branded the IOM Nimbus360, because it is a 360-degree view of the business for everyone. If someone asked for some information, the standard answer was 'It's on Nimbus360' (rather than email it to them). You then quickly made sure it was on there to reinforce the behaviour.

Wish we'd got it sorted at the beginning – but too late now?

Some companies were lucky enough[4] to have the IOM bedded down before they started to grow explosively – and put in place the procedures and disciplines to keep it up to date. Luck or foresight? Some of our clients, typically those in the telecommunications sector, recognised the value of the IOM to support the growth and therefore made it central to their launch plans.

One international telecommunications company took the

[3]Geoffrey Moore has written the marketing bible for technology companies, called *Crossing the Chasm*, and a follow-up book called *Inside the Tornado*.

[4]Hindsight (being 20:20 vision) can make you pretty smug... but only if you have spent the time keeping the content current. Going through massive expansion means that organisation structures, core processes, country operations and supplier relationships all change.

IOM and made it their blueprint for launching each new mobile phone operation in a new country. They estimated that it saved four months in launching the new operation and also $1million in fees normally paid to consultants. Multiply that by six countries and it can make a significant difference.

Alternatively, companies are looking to grow by acquisition. Here the IOM has been used to rapidly get the acquired company to work in a way consistent with its new parent. This is an interesting approach – the IOM is used to enable a far better assessment of the viability of the acquisition, making the due diligence much more than just a financial assessment. But that is the subject of another book...

The perfect time to start

For those who are drowning, or at best floundering, there is still hope. There is no perfect time to start. Waiting for the perfect time means that you will have even more employees and therefore greater adoption problems. It seems a difficult task when there are so many short-term priorities, but this is building long-term value and these results are not immediately apparent. It doesn't seem as important as new customers and new orders. It is not, but if it is planned in it can still be realised alongside these pressures.

Therefore you need to find a current initiative for which you can develop the IOM. It might be a software package implementation, a merger or acquisition, fixing a current set of problems, or the push to become compliant.

If none of these exist – then just get started.

 If you haven't got a reason to get started – then create a crisis.

A number of examples show that it can work for you, even in an industry that has been threatened by the global downturn. Look at Nokia: less than a decade ago, Nokia was hardly known. Today it is one of the world's leading innovators in the field of mobile communications. In the last few years, the company has experienced explosive growth in terms of both profit and headcount. Phil Brown, while Managing Director of Nokia Belgium, found that a clear and stable set of corporate values allowed them to achieve such phenomenal growth and become the magnet for talent that they are today. For Phil Brown, these values are mainly recruiting, training and motivation.

So the key message is that if you are about to expand – get the IOM in place NOW. If you are in the midst of rapid expansion – devote some time to getting the top-level strategy correct as this will help you prioritise the areas you need to focus on.

An example

Managing organic growth in the telecommunications industry

An American company and a Dutch mobile communications giant joined forces to launch a pan-European DSL provider. The start-up team faced aggressive and rapid growth targets, with one of the major challenges being controlling an unprecedented volume of transactions and orders. They needed a faster, more flexible and more effective way of capturing new business procedures from start to finish, and they needed the flexibility to adapt as the company progressed.

The team adopted the approach outlined in this book in defining business processes to create an overall graphical view of the entire company's operations – the IOM. Because it was available on every desktop and the whole company was working from the same perspective, changes and improvements were made more quickly and efficiently than they could ever have been without the IOM. As a result, having a complete overview saved countless hours, effort and money during the start-up, from producing system requirements right through to recruitment and staff training.

A key measure of the success was that the company was

further ahead after six months than its parent had been in the US after two years. Changes and improvements were made more quickly and efficiently, greatly reducing start-up timescales and costs.

Another example

Growing an international business against huge competitors

Critical to Europe's specialist internet datacentre provider and hosting company is the level of customer service. The company provides more than 200 customers across Europe with facilities management in multi-carrier datacentres. 'If our customers have a problem, we can get back to them within five minutes, compared with an industry average of four hours,' says the CEO.

Since launching, the company has enjoyed continued organic growth through a combination of providing the very best product and service for its customers and keeping its running costs to a minimum. Sales have rocketed over 600% a year from annualised sales of £100,000 to £6m three years later. This is an impressive record, but the company faces the challenges of managing rapid growth.

The management team needed to make sure that their management systems were optimised. From the outset, they knew that a paper-based system was not going to deliver. The Vice President of Customer Operations was tasked with implementing a solution that they could use to build an Electronic Management System – their name for the IOM. The criteria for the candidate software were resilience, usability and presentability.

The benefits that the approach brought are:

- Presentability. The graphical representation of processes and procedures means that it is instantly more usable than textual documents.

- Compliance. The process management approach means that management system (IOM) immediately complies with ISO 9000.

- Training. Staff training has become more straightforward. When a new recruit joins, they are given a road map to processes and procedures designed in the IOM.

- Control. Processes and procedures have been streamlined across all European locations. The Head Office management team retains control over the processes throughout the entire company.

- Speed to market. When making acquisitions in Europe, it has simplified and speeded up the process of amalgamating the management systems, despite potential hurdles such as cultural issues and language differences. The result was that seven datacentres were launched in three years.

- Cost savings. In terms of time saving and workload efficiency, there were savings of one to two employees in each datacentre location, which represented £80,000–£120,000 per year across the group.

Chapter 16

Using scorecards to make sustainable improvements

'Not everything that counts is countable and not everything that is countable counts.'

Albert Einstein

On the green light, go...

A number of years ago, I was one of the IT Directors at the DSS, the UK Government Social Security organisation. I had 500 staff in eight locations and a budget of £40m. In my rather large office (protected by a fierce secretary in her outer office), I had a PC with an executive information system (EIS) with lots of traffic lights reporting on my organisation's performance.

This was leading-edge technology at the time, but I had no choice in setting the traffic lights or how the data that made them turn green, amber or red was compiled. A complex application powered by mainframes crunched numbers for weeks to produce a set of traffic lights that the senior Directors saw. But those traffic lights weren't connected to any of our project processes or to any other definition of activity. I had no way of knowing what to do to change the traffic light from red to green. So I simply accepted the green lights and used the amber and red lights as early warnings to prepare my excuses for the next management meeting.

Having an EIS that creates performance data that isn't connected to an organisation's activities is like trying to play a video game with a disconnected joystick. The game is still in play (people are still at work) but the joystick operator (management) can't influence the action.

The other issue with the EIS is that it was driven by lagging indicators – numbers like last month's or last quarter's sales figures or customer churn. Things can start to go wrong in a business well before the performance measure turns the traffic light red. Using metrics that measure past events is like driving while looking through the rear window.[1] You can easily miss the opportunity or threat on the road ahead until you're upon it.

My projects were managed by a weekly project management meeting – with their own set of numbers and graphs carefully prepared and massaged by a large team in the Project Office. Does any of this sound familiar? Today's improved technology means that data is produced more quickly and can come from more sources. <u>But this doesn't make it any more successful at delivering a better result</u>. If an improvement is needed to be able to catch up or hit a milestone, then my question was always the same: 'What are we going to do differently?' And 'Work harder' is not necessarily the correct answer.

Let me give you an example. I once worked on a team selected by the CFO of a communications company to identify cost savings throughout the organisation. Our efforts were reaping results until we got to the Corporate Services organisation – the people who ran facilities, purchasing and the mail room. We quickly got bogged down by issues such as how many times a day the mail was delivered and the impact on corporate productivity of reducing deliveries from three to two times a day – the results they were measured on. Trouble was that total savings from the mail room could amount to $100,000 at the most, yet we were looking for $20 million!

The Corporate Services people weren't behaving irrationally. They just figured that what the company was measuring must be important. I finally convinced them that we had to focus on what was important to the business and not in this case what was being measured.

[1] Like some parents driving monster 4x4s (SUVs) around the city filled with fighting kids.

Scorecards are showing up in every product

With increased access to data and the greater processing power of servers and PCs, every software vendor is adding scorecarding to its products. Why? It's a very compelling way to display metrics or numbers to the top executive team – and that's the level at which every vendor wants to sell its software.[2]

There is no doubt that there is a demand for timely and accurate information rather than just data. With the right information, better decisions can be made. Decisions are more effective when they are made quickly in response to a business problem. They are also more effective when they are disseminated throughout the organisation so that appropriate action is taken. Scorecarding software systems can make good decision-making much easier by providing comprehensive information.

Think how changes in technology have altered the way we get information. The company where I work operates with an infrastructure linking its overseas office with its headquarters in the UK, which just five years ago was only within the financial reach of a multinational conglomerate. I can sit in my office in the UK, in my home office, in our offices in New York, or in a client's meeting room in the Netherlands and have the same level of secure, rapid access to my company's system and email and a view of my company's real-time performance.

But this doesn't make the system as such any more useful at delivering a better result.

Except that in our company I can look at the scorecards, and if there is an issue I can link directly to the processes which affect and influence those metrics. From there I can see who is accountable for those processes, the current work in progress to improve them, and the history of past performance. I am, of course, navigating my way around our IOM.

---

[2]You may call this cynical – but a cynic is what an optimist calls a realist.

Metrics in the correct context

Every book on scorecarding will tell you that you need to measure the right things – which are not always easily measured. But what they don't tell you is that you need to present the measures within the context of their processes. If you don't, then the owner of the metric can see that they are doing well or badly – but have no way of knowing what to do more of if they are doing well, or what to change if they are doing badly.

The other issue is that metrics are interrelated – several measures together affect a third measure. Unless the interactions in terms of activities (process) are understood, then the right corrective action is impossible to apply.

The question is whether the definition of process or metrics comes first – and this is discussed in Chapter 8. But if you're reading this chapter then you are probably in the midst of a scorecarding project, possibly driven by one of the large Business Intelligence vendors. So what can you do?

How to integrate the IOM with your scorecarding initiative

If you have a scorecarding initiative in full flood with timescales to hit, how can you get better value from it? Clearly, putting the IOM in place will allow the team to put the metrics they are defining into some context. More importantly, this will validate that the metrics being defined are the correct ones.

When you find that the team are struggling to define some of the metrics because the end users are unclear about their detailed processes, then this is the time to step in. The IOM will be a massive help. The project team and the end users can work together to define the correct metrics – this will also start the adoption of the scorecards into the organisation.

Talking to an implementation consultant about the principles of the IOM was enlightening. He suddenly got

very excited as he recognised that this was what he was
searching for when helping clients define the metrics on his
scorecarding projects.[3]

---

[3]He got so excited that he applied to join our company.

PART IV: Simple steps to success

Introduction

The principles that I've described in this book seem simple. Trivially simple, in fact. They make a lot of common sense. But have you noticed that common sense, sadly, is not really that common at all?[1]

I'm almost sure this is what we are doing

I guess many of you are thinking that these approaches are already being employed in your project, your division, your company. Or you hope that they are. Can you be 100% sure? So why not find out if they really are?

 Look at your post-project review reports and match the REAL savings/benefits against those put up in the business case to get the project launched.

So, can you see from some of your own examples why some of your initiatives did not receive the benefits anticipated that were signed off in the business case?

None of the clients my company works with is getting zero benefits. They all have initiatives being run by conscientious teams who are striving to get the best for their companies. However, our approach, driven around the principle of an IOM, can give them greater benefits.

Learning by example

The examples and case studies I've given in this book are real – but the question is 'Can I apply this and make it work for my project, for my division, for my company?' The purpose of this section of the book is to understand what those other successful companies did – how they ran their projects and how they organised themselves. I will also explain what the focus of the project was and what were the key steps they took. Finally, I recognise that your project may not be a greenfield site. You haven't got a clean sheet of paper. This isn't the only thing you have to worry about.

---

[1] Just take a look at the recent US litigation. Suing for being scalded by hot coffee, suing for tripping over a child in a sofa shop (her OWN child).

Your executives and team members are no doubt fully occupied with current projects, initiatives and existing workloads. In addition, you'll have multiple projects in process; a business to run; customers, shareholders and employees to satisfy; plus existing technology investments. And I bet you have a smaller budget than last year, yet you're still expected to achieve more. That's business.

I can hear you saying 'The last thing you need now is another distraction and another change in direction.' But this isn't a distraction or diversion – this is leveraging what you are already doing

I have asked Richard Parker, Senior Vice President Sales and Implementation at my company, to take you through the 'Nimbus Performance Management Methodology (PMM) – 5 Steps to Adoption'. He has first-hand experience of this as he spends the majority of his time working with clients to apply the principles of the Intelligent Operations Manual (IOM) and help drive more value from their initiatives.

In the following chapters Richard takes a closer look at each step that drives adoption. There isn't space for an in-depth discussion about each step, the pros and cons, various hints and tips, estimating approaches, resourcing requirements or lots of anecdotes. That is the topic of a far more detailed book... Or, alternatively the PMM is available as an IOM.

Instead, he intends to give you a high-level understanding of the key activities within each step, what is being delivered and some elements to be aware of in terms of adoption and risk.

This is not a detailed methodology. Bearing in mind that it needs to fit alongside the current initiative that you are running, it needs to complement it. There is a sequence which we believe works best – hence the numbering – and if you get all the way to Step 5 you will get better adoption and therefore greater benefits than if you only complete up to Step 3. If you don't at least complete Step 2, you don't have an IOM.

The chapters that follow and outline each step have the same structure:

- how this helps adoption
- summary of the key activities
- discussion of each activity
- issues to be aware of
- deliverables from this step.

Chapter 17

Step-by-step approach

'Screw it. Let's do it.'

Richard Branson

Getting real results from your initiatives means establishing an IOM, giving access to all the stakeholders, putting in place the mechanism and culture to maintain it, and then reusing it on subsequent initiatives. That is what drives adoption.

From the experience of countless client engagements I have identified five simple steps. These steps build on everything that we have discussed in the previous chapters, but set them out in a practical blueprint for ACTION.

 Actions speak louder than words.

I suggest that you read this chapter through quickly, and then refer back to it as you read the subsequent chapters to put them into context.

So let's take a look at a summary of each step.

STEP 1 – Launch the project

For some companies this is the vision or mission. But it is more than that, as explained in chapter 2. We've all seen mission statements like 'To be the leading provider of healthcare'. The objectives need to be measurable and members of the top team accountable for them, such as 'Launch in 3 new regions next year... Cut costs by 15% in

US... Increase margin by 13% over the next 3 years'. And, as we said earlier, these tell you what the company wants to achieve, but still do not describe which is the most important.

You also need shared agreement from the executive team as to the operations strategy of the business. It is the end-to-end process of the company to achieve those objectives. This may be the top team if you're looking at the whole business, or it may be the top level of an operating unit, or of a plant. The key is using the same common language as the rest of the company. Thrashing out this simple picture in a workshop can be most illuminating. All the duplication, holes and inconsistencies between teams headed by each executive member become (painfully) visible, when described as a high-level visual diagram showing end-to-end processes in an IOM.

Finally, you need to give the IOM a strong brand identity. Names we've seen work are How2, Excellence Online (EOL), PACE (Process, Alignment, Control & Execution), Nimbus360, MyToyota.

STEP 2 – Analyse the business

This can be a major undertaking in a large company, and I suggest you start from the top level, even if the work currently applies to a specific initiative, as it sets the context for the initiative. The priority for development of lower levels will be clear from the alignment of goals, objectives and high-level KPIs with the activities and ownership on the top-level diagram.

Start by taking each activity at the top level you want to expand and use similar workshops to drill down until you read the level where work gets done. At this point you are defining, or linking to, Procedures or Work Instructions – and the forms, templates, documents and enterprise applications needed to get the job done.

You have created a pictorial, online operations manual, that not only explains what needs to be done, but also has all the tools, applications, information and help to be able to do it – all in the same place – at the point of need.

When you have completed Step 2 you have an IOM which may cover only one area of the business based on the initiative it is supporting. Over time it will be completed for other areas of the business as other initiatives reuse it. Alternatively, when you discover the benefits of having the IOM in place you may make it an initiative in its own right.

Don't worry if the IOM describes only a part of your operation at this point. The IOM is never 'complete' – to be most valuable it is a living, decentralised, ever-changing part of your business fabric.

But... if you haven't already completed Step 1 then there will be no alignment between the corporate goals and the day-to-day activities of your staff.

STEP 3 – Personalise the IOM to make it relevant

This means making the IOM available to all staff, wherever they are[1]. Fortunately, the company intranet and the internet make this possible at viable cost in a secure environment – even for the smallest company. Access to corporate information is now possible in offices, at home over broadband, on client sites out through their network onto the internet, using WiFi in cafés and clubs.

Giving people the ability to access the information is the first step. Making the content worth accessing is the second.

No one wants to look at process maps. What they want is help on 'how to' do a particular activity, which will flow across multiple diagrams and organisations. Therefore the information needs to be presented in an easily understood format – storyboards or 'guided tours'.

---

[1] Some of you probably remember the Martini advert: 'Any time, any place, any where – there's a wonderful joy you can share...' (Martini/The Single Source of Truth').

Finally the storyboards, documents, metrics and change actions of interest to an individual need to be presented onto their personalised page or team page on their intranet.

But if you haven't completed Step 2 then there isn't anything worth looking at.

STEP 4 – Deploy the model to the business

Implementing the IOM is similar to implementing any other product. People need to be trained. The rollout needs to be planned and communicated to the organisation, reinforcing the brand developed at Step 1. This is the critical part of Adoption. This is the sales job.

Once implemented you need to start catching people doing the right things and praise them, and identify and fix problems with adoption. This is all about making sure the initial experiences of IOM for end users is positive to spread its adoption virally.

Finally, an assessment of the results vs the objective is conducted to be able to close off the project. Now you are into continual improvement.

But if you haven't completed Step 3 then you're not ready to rollout the IOM . . . or whatever you call it.

STEP 5 – Operate and improve the business

Building the IOM is not the end goal. Using it to drive continuous improvement is. Therefore you need the mechanism for driving and controlling change is critical.

If that 'Single Source of Truth' does not have a SIMPLE, EASY method (remember – the path of least resistance) of being maintained, I can guarantee it won't be kept up to date. It will gather dust in a corner of the intranet in the same way the Quality Manual gathered dust on the shelves. You need to bear in mind that the people maintaining this information are not full-time 'administrators of the system' (unlike the Quality Team were for the Quality Manual). They are fully employed, and this is another activity in their already crowded schedule.

To add a level of complication, the changes need to be version-controlled and auditable (if you are getting the most out of your IOM), as they are critical to maintaining compliance. We know this is vital in regulated industries such as the pharmaceutical industry or in financial services. But it is equally important, I would argue, in any company. And when changes are made, then those affected need to be informed of and directed to the changes.

The following five chapters explore each step in more detail.

Chapter 18

Step 1: Launch the project

1 Launch   2 Analyse   3 Personalise   4 Deploy   5 Operate

How this helps adoption

- Leadership from the top with senior management sponsorship.

- Clear vision of how the senior team wants the business to operate in terms of end-to-end processes, priorities and measures.

- Strong branding of IOM.

Summary of activities

- Get the infrastructure and software in place to manage the IOM before you start.

- Understand existing initiatives and priorities, and agree the goals, CSFs and KPIs for the scope of the business you want to address.

- Conduct top-level workshop for future vision and link existing high-level metrics to high-level activities.

- Develop a baseline cost model.

- Establish alignment between objectives for initiatives, core processes, ownership and priorities.

- Brand the IOM.

- Ensure senior management communicate to their line management the importance of giving time to develop the detail of the IOM – without this, it will fail.

Discussion of each activity

- Install hardware and network infrastructure and software to manage the IOM. This includes giving access to all stakeholders from the earliest possible stage. Get the IT department involved early so that they understand what is required and allow the IOM onto production environment. If this is not possible, look for test environment or consider a hosted environment.

- Understand existing initiatives and priorities, and agree the goals, CSF and KPIs. What are the initiatives that are most critical to the organisation? A SAP implementation, integration of the recent merger or acquisition, supply chain cost reduction? This is the area which will be the primary focus for the development of the IOM. The goals, CSF and KPI will still be the global and divisional business objectives, but driven down to the detail and context of this initiative.

- Conduct top-level workshop for future vision and link existing high-level metrics to high-level activities. In many circumstances there will be no value in mapping the current state of the company – this is about transformational change. The high-level structure of the IOM is always more valuable when it articulates the senior management's vision of the way they would like to see the company. Even where the existing 'current state' operations have to be mapped as part of the initiative, it is usually more valuable to detail them below this future vision. Linking metrics will give direction and identify the priority for mapping the lower-level activities and identifying likely quick wins.

- Establish alignment between objectives for initiatives, core processes, ownership and priorities. You probably have multiple initiatives working independently, but this may be the first time you are able to see their relationships in driving the business forward. Ensure that senior management communicate to their line management the importance of giving time to develop the detail of the IOM – without this it will fail. Probably the greatest risk when developing the detail of the IOM is access to the right people. Senior management communicate best by example. If they delegate (or abdicate), then so will everyone else.

- The branding of the IOM is critical to buy-in. It needs to be memorable, something everyone can relate to and is simple. Get your marketing organisation involved. This is what they are good at. Develop a new logo, look and feel and communications programme which really SELLS the IOM to the organisation.

Key issues to be aware of

- IT departments are hesitant about installing new software applications in a short time frame. It will lessen adoption if the infrastructure is not in place from the start of the top-level workshop. External hosting of the IOM software may be an option.

- Access to key people when their focus may be elsewhere. The value of the information in the IOM is based on the quality of the input. The output from a workshop with a key person absent will not be agreed or accepted – leading to poor adoption.

- The top-level workshop will need external facilitation – a 'stranger with a briefcase'. An employee or sub-contractor will be too aware of their continued employment to be able to speak freely to the top team to get the right results. Knowledge of the business is not a prerequisite. The ability to ask awkward and obvious questions can be immensely valuable.

- The company culture is focused on functions or departments and not on end-to-end processes. This is driven from the top of the organisation. Is there a desire to drive the business from a process focus? Is there a perceived benefit in doing so? If not, focus should be placed purely on those areas that require such a focus like a recognised cross-functional problem. An example might be 'Quote to Cash' or 'Idea to Product' to deliver results and open people's minds.

- Defining ownership of processes that cross functional boundaries. Related to the previous point, a process can have only one owner, but may span departments. Ownership is best seen as the person responsible for the performance of the end-to-end process – not the people within it.

- There is no agreed strategy, or multiple strategies at multiple levels, or the implications of the strategy are not understood below the top level of management. The top-level workshop will require a meaningful set of objectives and key metrics as a starting point for prioritisation and decisions around many aspects of operational focus.

- Organisations find it easy to start defining processes at a low level. They see 'results' (i.e. process maps appear), but as they are not developed within the context of the top-level diagram they do not fit as part of an end-to-end process. When people start mapping against local agendas at lower levels, the result is myriad overlaps and gaps within the IOM.

Deliverables from this Step

- Objectives articulated in enough detail to enable individual sub-level processes to be designed to achieve them

- Top level structure of IOM, which is the top diagram and the immediate sub-levels, each with:
  - activities identified
  - scope of each activity defined, which is the input and output
  - ownership and review/sign-off of each activity defined
  - key metrics associated with each activity
  - documents, applications and forms attached to each activity

- Agreed priorities for the development of lower levels

- Agreement from line management to ensure staff are available to attend lower-level workshops

Chapter 19

Step 2: Analyse the business

1 Launch   **2 Analyse**   3 Personalise   4 Deploy   5 Operate

How this helps adoption

- Commitment of senior management is understood through actions like a five-minute kickoff at the start of key live workshops.

- Common agreement from attendees of each lower-level workshop directly impacts upon adoption at every stage.

- Momentum and involvement is maintained through online feedback, review and sign-off immediately after the workshops.

Summary of activities

- Develop consistent guidelines and common language.

- Conduct live workshops to develop lower-level diagrams.

- Cascade live process ownership by role against activities, NOT by department or function.

- Connect measures to activities and tie into roles and responsibilities.

- Drive feedback, review and sign-off immediately after the workshops via the intranet to maintain momentum.

Discussion of each activity

- Develop consistent guidelines and common language. Strict adherence to a simple diagramming standard is critical to make every diagram consistent and easily understood. This will need to be policed as part of the sign-off. The simple building block described earlier in this book (see page 60) is the key to this.

- Conduct live process workshops to develop lower levels. The scope of the workshop is taken from the input and output of the parent activity. It is critical to have workshop attendees who can represent all activities from input to output. If any are missing or have sent representatives with no decision-making ability the workshop will not reach consensus and shared agreement.

- Cascade ownership by roles against activities, NOT departments or functions. As discussed in chapter 6, adoption is tied to ownership and the feeling of responsibility. It cannot start too early. Therefore every diagram should have a credible process owner who is responsible for the maintenance and improvement of the process, and measured by the performance of that process. They are not necessarily responsible for all the staff who use those processes.

- Connect measures to activities and tie into roles and responsibilities. A key part of the process is how it is measured. Those metrics should be presented attached to the activities that drive them. This level of accountability increases adoption because it makes the diagrams a decision-making tool for managers as well as an operations guide for the 'shop floor'. It also ties metrics both to the activities that produce them and to the people in the roles that can impact the metrics. The visibility and accountability that this provides is exceptional.

- Drive feedback, review and sign-off immediately after the workshops via the intranet to maintain momentum. Aim to reduce the time from workshop to final sign-off by using the collaborative review and sign-off features of the IOM. This will build pace and momentum, giving people confidence that this is more than 'another two-year process definition project'. It also allows stakeholders who could not attend to give input without joining the endless 'review of the notes and documentation of the meeting I missed'. This point alone has saved man months of time on projects.

Key issues to be aware of

- Access to the correct-level people – the ONLY challenge.

- Process ownership – the content has to be owned, not just obeyed.

- Not using live workshops – collating content from interviews or previous exercises does not build a shared agreement and ownership, which is where adoption starts.

- People at lower levels not understanding the context of what is going on with this 'IOM' thing. The key here is good communication, a strong direction from senior management and a meaningful, useful top level to provide context and clarity of purpose.

Deliverables from this Step

- Lower-level process diagrams, each with:
  - activities identified
  - scope of each activity defined, which is the input and output
  - ownership and review/sign-off of each activity defined
  - key metrics associated with each activity
  - documents, applications, forms attached to each activity
- Continued communication from senior management and access to the people needed to develop further and maintain content.

Chapter 20

Step 3: Personalise the IOM and make it relevant

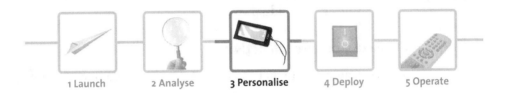

1 Launch   2 Analyse   **3 Personalise**   4 Deploy   5 Operate

How this helps adoption

- By establishing the infrastructure for the IOM early in the project, access and buy-in starts immediately after the top-level workshop.

- If senior people are seen to use the IOM in context of initiatives and day to day management, it will be seen as the 'Single Source of Truth'.

- People get to see what they do in the context of the business, and corporate strategy, probably for the first time.

- People are not introduced to change – they are part of creating it.

- First impressions count – you want to get internal viral marketing of the value of the IOM.

Summary of activities

- Demonstrate that the IOM is the 'Single Source of Truth' and will be the mechanism for collaboration and continuous improvement.

- Ensure key stakeholders are given access and are able to receive email notifications.

- Identify operational owners/authors for diagrams and prepare them to transfer ownership at the earliest opportunity.

- Establish approach to define roles for activities and link roles to individual users.

Discussion of each activity

- Demonstrate that the IOM is the 'Single Source of Truth' and is the mechanism for collaboration and continuous improvement. If the information is not maintained through a collaborative effort by the process owners it will not remain relevant and correct, and adoption will fade. It will become yet another dead source of 'content' on the corporate intranet. We've all seen initiatives stall and die because nobody trusts the information to be accurate and up to date.

- Ensure key stakeholders are given access and are able to receive email notifications. The IT department should ensure that 'single sign-on' is set up, so that PC log-on credentials are used to allow access to the IOM. While it may seem a small issue, experience shows that multiple log-ons are a huge barrier to adoption. This has to be simple, seamless and a useful (not annoying) part of the everyday desktop.

- Identify operational owners/authors for diagrams and transfer ownership at the earliest opportunity. If end users start to use and maintain their information on the IOM they will begin to feel some ownership.

This is reinforced by the accountability and measurement of the process. People will need to be trained on how to maintain and improve their part of the IOM as a small part of their day job, but the results and returns massively outweigh the investment.

- Define roles for activities and link roles to individual users. You are then able to dynamically create people's job descriptions based on the roles they currently have in the organisation. This drives much closer attention as to who actually does what and supports a wealth of improvement initiatives. Clearly, this is best when it involves HR from an early stage.

Key issues to be aware of

- Resistance by IT to put LDAP (single sign-on) in place. To deliver the major quick and long-term wins, the IOM needs to be seamlessly accessible to everyone via the intranet.

- The organisation is not capable of integrating process ownership, role-based thinking, or dynamic activity-based thinking into their operation.

- Too much focus on the local objective, missing the big opportunities for the IOM to impact the whole business. Alternatively, there is too much focus on the big picture, so 'quick win' opportunities are missed which would otherwise drive momentum and buy-in. The trick is to include both, and deliver on both.

- Lip service to buy-in, workshops and proper engagement reduces adoption of the IOM.

Deliverables from this Step

- The IOM has an identity, and it is seen as a valuable asset. It is recognised as the 'Single Source of Truth', and senior management are committed to its development and maintenance.

- Access over the intranet is set up for all stakeholders with single sign-on and linked to email.

- Ownership and priority of key lower levels is defined.

- The concept of 'roles' is defined and ready to be linked to individual users during development of the IOM.

Chapter 21

Step 4: Deploy the model to the business

1 Launch   2 Analyse   3 Personalise   **4 Deploy**   5 Operate

How this helps adoption

- Training reinforces the benefits of a common approach and ensures end users' initial experience is positive.

- Responsive to changes when problems are found so reinforces viral word of mouth communication.

- Proactive support and monitoring of the IOM encourages adoption (stick and carrot).

Summary of activities

- Deliver training.

- Launch IOM rollout.

- Assess usage of IOM and survey users for feedback.

- Drive formal programme of updates based on feedback.

- Assess value of IOM.

Discussion of each activity

- Training is not just end users. It is also their line managers, who are often the greatest barrier to change. They may see that IOM as a threat, as additional work or just irrelevant. They need to understand that it is a tool to make their jobs easier.

- The launch should be well planned and executed, and high profile. Everyone should understand that the IOM is here to stay and is not just another management fad or initiative.

- Establish that staff are following the IOM, and if not, identify what changes are required. Use the IOM user logs to establish access patterns. The IOM is about continuous improvement driven by process owners because it delivers them value and is achievable. If the IOM is not used, then why not? Work out what should change – the information in the IOM, the incentives, the culture and behaviours, the sponsorship?

- Integrate IOM with existing regulatory standards and any internal/external auditing practices. This should happen naturally as the IOM will support any regulatory initiative, but any regulatory documentation needs linking into the IOM. Ensure that internal quality and external auditing staff are educated about the value and purpose of the IOM before they create unnecessary duplication or additional content.

- Define key risk/control points and ensure that these are regularly/appropriately audited. These can be overlaid on the processes as part of the IOM, dramatically reducing the effort to meet regulations such as Sarbanes-Oxley and Basel II. Frequently, companies have used the IOM to drive reporting on performance into management meetings.

- Measure the use and adoption of the IOM itself. As the IOM is most usually a web-based system, the simple measure of 'page hits' can tell a lot about the organisation's use of it. In addition, looking at who is using specific control points and following certain standards can be enormously important.

Key issues to be aware of

- Non-attendance at training.
- Lack of support or funding by senior management at launch.
- Initiatives fail due to lack of change control – non-compliant chaos.
- Initiatives fail due to unnecessary change 'administrivia' – locked-down and inflexible, and therefore not used.
- Too much rigour (where not genuinely required for compliance) will kill adoption every time.

Deliverables from this Step

- IOM launched.
- Users trained.
- A clearly defined change management cycle.
- Audit trail of changes.
- BAU (Business As Usual – IOM is part of fabric of organisation).

Chapter 22

Step 5: Operate and improve the business

1 Launch 2 Analyse 3 Personalise 4 Deploy **5 Operate**

How this helps adoption

- If the IOM is valuable and up to date it will be used – again and again. If it is not current it will die in weeks, not months.

- Used as an operation guide for junior staff it will be valuable. Used as a performance tool for senior staff it will be invaluable.

Summary of activities

- Review process indicators.

- Capture and publish performance data.

- Review performance gaps as actions.

- Change the process or the people.

- Review KPIs monthly.

Discussion of each activity

- Validate the current measures are correct at every level i.e. leading indicators, and not just the lagging indicators or those that are easy to measure. Measuring everything is as bad as measuring nothing. Determining the correct measure is not necessarily easy, but is nigh on impossible if you do not understand the operational context or end-to-end process up to this point.

- Determine new process-focused management reporting of measures. The current reporting may need to change as old functionally structured measures are scrapped and new activity-focused measures created.

- Line managers/HR reward individuals according to performance against measures in context of activities. If the processes and measures are aligned with the objectives of the company why wouldn't you offer incentives (give recognition, promote, pay bonuses) to staff to excel. This doesn't often happen at present because there is misalignment or lack of understanding of which activities have the impact on which key metrics, and who should be responsible for their performance.

- Use change management techniques to change the process or to get better adoption (i.e. change the people). Typical techniques are Six Sigma or Lean Sigma.

- Use the KPIs and processes to assess your performance. Use both together to set the agenda for change and prioritise actions.

Key issues to be aware of

- If you drive measures and process initiatives separately they are inherently misaligned, so often drive dysfunctional behaviour.

- Measurement initiatives tend to be driven by 'numbers' people – who don't really understand process, so they need to be educated about the powerful relationship.

- Senior management focus on the KPIs rather than KPIs and processes. A drop in performance often results in calls for 'better performance', 'more focus' etc., but should drive a review of the activity in context of process.

- Feedback/changes are not initiated or driven through IOM but by informal routes which means the valuable audit trail is lost. This will compromise SOX and ISO accreditations.

- Unless proactively managed, all organisations will revert to type and respond to new requirements (e.g. system implementations) with old habits – e.g. business requirement specified in MSWord documents even though the processes are already all in the IOM. This is where senior management needs to 'lead from the front' and force teams to justify why they are NOT using the IOM.

- Teams will often go for the easy life. If a big Systems Integrator is demanding a particular format or way of documenting then this often determines the project documentation in parallel to the IOM – despite expense, duplication, wasted resources, etc.

Deliverables from this Step

- There are none, this is a continuous cycle! But seriously, the results are update processes and KPIs.

Part V: Tools

Chapter 23

Am I ready for this?
Test yourself

'More things are lost by indecision, than by wrong decision, so you are ready before you know. Just do it!'

Anon

I thought it might be useful for you to be able to assess whether you are in a position to take advantage of the principles of the IOM. I suppose this question could have been posed in the first chapter, but then if the answer had been 'No', you wouldn't have needed to read this book. However, in my experience there are very few situations where the answer is a definite 'No'. If you aren't able to implement the IOM as we've described, I'm sure that the earlier chapters will, at the very least, have got you thinking about business transformation in a different way.

So, here are a few questions (which I've listed under different categories) to find out if you are really ready to implement this approach. The questionnaire is the style of an 'Are you a sensitive lover?' type of quiz, found in popular magazines. At the end you can add up your scores and, based on your total, I've suggested some things to think about.

Try this simple quiz to find out if you are really ready for it by answering the multiple-choice questions and then totting up your score…

NEED – Do I need this? Some typical signs...

Question 1: Do you have one or more business transformation initiatives?

    a. Yes, they are co-ordinated by a Programme Office with a shared business model

    b. No, but there is one major initiative across the company

    c. Yes, but we seem to have difficulty co-ordinating the results

    d. I've no idea. Each department does its own thing.

Question 2: How many of the following initiatives are being run by your company: enterprise application implementation (ERP, CRM, Supply Chain), Six Sigma, Business Process Reengineering, Sarbanes-Oxley, M&A integration, outsourcing/shared services, launching new operations...?

    a. One or none

    b. Between two and four

    c. More than four

    d. Probably all of them.

Question 3: What percentage of the benefits stated in the business case for each initiative do you actually achieve?

    a. 75–100%

    b. 50–75%

    c. Less than 50%

    d. We don't ever measure the benefits.

DESIRE – Is there a strong enough desire to follow through?

Question 4: How is your positioning against the competition best described?

    a. We are setting the pace of change for others to follow

b. We are able respond to change and to stay competitive

c. We are able respond to change but at a huge cost

d. We are unable to respond quickly enough.

Question 5: Does your ability to stay alive require you to transform the business?

a. No – we need some small course corrections

b. Yes – but it is limited to one business unit

c. Yes – we recognise that changes are required

d. Yes – we require a radical overhaul of the business model.

Question 6: Do the top team and managers recognise the benefits of moving to a process-focused approach?

a. We have aligned our organisation chart to the cross-functional processes

b. We have process owners and a functional organisation chart

c. Work is organised in line with the functional organisation chart

d. Getting managers in different departments to talk would be a first.

Question 7: Which of these statements best reflects your attitude to compliance?

a. It is imperative and my company has to achieve the highest levels of compliance

b. It's a necessary evil

c. It can sometimes get in the way of business

d. I wonder who will get found out next?

OPPORTUNITY – Are there initiatives where this could be applied now?

Question 8: Can you see any initiative where you could apply these principles?

a. We already have a central source of information reused by all initiatives

b. We have a perfect initiative starting in the next month – the business case is being presented at the next Board meeting

c. I can see an opportunity in the next three–six months

d. I'd need the management team and project managers to read this book before I'd get them to adopt these ideas.

Question 9: Can you mandate this approach on your external consultants?

a. We mandate a process-focused approach in all projects

b. We have a good relationship with our consultants and they are open to new ideas

c. We would need to convince the consultants of the benefits of this approach

d. We have fixed-price contracts; they will fleece us if we try to change.

Question 10: How much is your business controlled by regulatory bodies?

a. Very little – thankfully

b. As we have a US parent we need to comply with Sarbanes-Oxley

c. We need to comply with our industry regulations (e.g. FSA for Financial Services, FDA for Pharmaceuticals)

d. You name it – we've got it. It seems like we work for the compliance offices.

CAPABILITY – Do you have the technical infrastructure and the skills?

Question 11: How well connected is your organisation?

a. All our offices are connected by a single intranet and many of our staff have full access to servers and systems from home

b. All our offices are connected by a single intranet

c. We have separate intranets for each country

d. We are thinking of outsourcing this area of IT.

Question 12: How long does it take to get a new software application installed?

a. With a business sponsor, less than a month. That is the IT department's SLA

b. Less than a month on a test server, and less than three months into production

c. It varies a lot based on IT's priorities – you put it in the queue and wait

d. We've outsourced IT to Company X so it is now impossible.

Question 13: What experience is there of running process-focused projects?

a. We are currently running all projects using the principles in this book

b. We have a project manager who has the skills and a small team of analysts

c. We have strong project skills, but would need coaching and support

d. This would be a first. We would have to depend on external consultants.

LEADERSHIP – Is there support at senior management to become process-focused?

Question 14: Do you have a single strategy in place which aligns the top team?

    a. Yes. We couldn't perform without it

    b. Yes. We reached agreement on a strategy in the end

    c. Yes. I think so

    d. Yes. In fact we have several of them (and we'll probably have a new one next week).

Question 15: How many of your top team would openly endorse the principles in the book?

    a. Virtually all of them. A couple of them could have written the book

    b. Certainly the operational side – the finance team have a numbers basis

    c. Very few, but after they've read it they would be open to the approach

    d. Forget it. They are too busy fighting turf wars.

Question 16: What chance is there of changing the organisation structure around the end-to-end processes?

    a. We're nearly there

    b. We'd be more comfortable with a matrix organisation reconciling functions with processes

    c. We've a strong functional organisation and we'd need to be convinced of the benefits

    d. Didn't you see my answer to Q15? No way.

Question 17: If you were to receive an award for your desk, which one of these phrases would be engraved:

    a. 'The buck stops here'

    b. 'Executive of the year'

c. 'It was like that when I found it'

d. 'Gone for lunch – back in 2015'.

Interpreting your score

Now simply add up your scores (with or without the help of your accountant, as necessary).

For every 'a' you score 10 points; every 'b' = 8 points; every 'c' = 5 points; every 'd' = 0 points. How have you done? How ready are you for it?

Over 120 points:

Great – you're red-hot. Give me a call because I'd love to profile your success story on our website and in the next book. I'm really excited you are proving the principles outlined in this book.

80–120 points:

You're nearly ready to take the plunge, but there are still a few things you need to sort out. At least you are aware that some things need to change. Think through all of the issues raised in this book and, once you've done that, you can leap right in.

30–79 points:

Unless you get a lot more buy-in for the principles any initiative is likely to fail. It sounds like you need a bulk order of the book so you can distribute it more widely – or get the top team to attend one of my seminars.

0–29 points:

You're clearly passionate about the process-focused approach or you wouldn't have read this far, but clearly you are in the wrong company. Come and talk to us because we know some companies that need you. At the very least, get out now before the excitement in you dies.

Chapter 24

Questions to ask your team

'Learn to love what you've been taught to fear.
Act more quickly, Find more value. Always look for the
upside. See that change is opportunity's nickname'.
Hewlett-Packard

So you have set your strategy and want to execute it successfully by involving every person and every part of your business. In order to do so, you need the right technology and you may be bombarded, overloaded or just plain baffled by your own team, the consultants who are advising them and the software vendors who are trying to sell to them.

Therefore I've listed some questions to ask at different stages of the initiative to test whether you're likely to get the benefits that are being claimed. The stages are:

1. the presentation of the business case

2. the early scoping of the initiative

3. the initiative's development

4. the roll-out of the results of the initiative to the company.

1. During the presentation of the business case

- How does this initiative reconcile with corporate strategy and objectives?

- How are initiative A and initiative B going to work consistently?

- What are the priorities?

- What does adoption mean to you?

- What is the cost and risk of failure, and how are we measuring success?

- How will this initiative integrate with our existing systems?

- How are we using the existing Intelligent Operations Manual?

- Are Systems Integrators (SI)/consultants incentivised by our success/adoption?

- What methodology/tools/approach are SI/consultants recommending – and have we mandated a process-led approach?

- Are we using the correct software tools to actively manage the IOM – i.e. more than MSOffice or a process mapping tool?

- Do we have IT's support to put the infrastructure for the IOM in place prior to starting the project?

- Have you read *Common Approach – Uncommon Results?*

2. During the early scoping of the initiative

- When is the top-level workshop, who is attending and is anyone abstaining?

- What is the scope of the initiative and who is signing it off?

- How are initiative A and initiative B going to work consistently?

- How will we gain an understanding of the power of adoption/process/IOM throughout the project team and sponsors?

- How have we set the priorities?

- What are the quick wins expected to get early success and build momentum?
- How have we measured pre-initiative adoption?
- Has IT put the infrastructure for IOM in place?
- Are SI/consultants incentivised in our success/adoption?
- Have you read *Common Approach – Uncommon Results?*

3. During the initiative's development

- How is this initiative impacting the other initiatives in the company?
- Are we using the existing IOM?
- Does everyone have intranet access to the IOM – easily and simply?
- How is the process-driven approach being accepted?
- Is there still sponsorship at a senior level for the initiative and approach?
- Are the correct people being made available for workshops?
- Down to what level have we documented the processes?
- Are we seeing increased (measurable) adoption?
- Are SI/consultants incentivised in our success/adoption?
- Have you read *Common Approach – Uncommon Results?*

4. During the roll-out of the results of the initiative to the company

- What is our strategy for driving greater adoption through roll-out?

- What are the barriers to adoption?

- Does everyone have intranet access to the IOM – easily and simply?

- Are SI/consultants incentivised in our success/adoption?

- Are we seeing increased (measurable) adoption?

- How is this initiative integrating with our existing systems?

- Have you read *Common Approach – Uncommon Results?*

Chapter 25

Running senior-level workshops

'Business today is about nuts and bolts, the mechanics of making companies work.'

Michael Hammer – *Author of* Reengineering the Corporation *and* The Agenda

Fundamental to the success of the approach described in this book are workshops where the processes are developed in a software tool, LIVE on screen. They cannot be beaten for speed and achieving consensus, and they stimulate both adoption and momentum.

No other medium will allow you to gather the key people in a room (not a separate committee), and immediately agree on the spot that what is on the screen is indeed what everyone will do from now on.

The alternatives won't achieve any of these benefits.

- Analysts interviewing individuals and presenting the report collectively is slow, time-consuming, does not get consensus and fundamentally does not engender adoption.

- Workshops on whiteboards (where a scribe writes it up at the end of the session and distributes it for comment) are better, but fail for one critical reason. Whatever is written up can never look exactly the same as what appeared on the whiteboards because it ends up on a screen. Therefore you lose adoption.

The only way to conduct the workshop is by using a process management software application that is quick enough to use live. That means it has the ability to draw lines, boxes, drill down, link to documents and tidy up and format the diagrams in a way that is so user-friendly that it does not disrupt the flow of the workshop. This ensures that you get agreement and sign-off at the end of the workshop, and what the workshop participants see on screen is what appears on the intranet when they get back to their offices.

There is clearly more preparation required for a first top-level workshop compared with lower-level workshops, as you would start with a blank screen. Lower-level workshops already have the context (scope) and metrics (objectives) set from the diagram above.

Finally, as you break down to lower levels, the workshops become smaller and faster. The top-level workshop normally takes the best part of a day, depending on the politics and education on process-thinking required for the top team. The next level is quicker – normally half a day. As you get to the level of diagram where the real work gets done, it could be just two people sitting around a PC.

Below I have summarised, in check-list format, some key elements to make these live workshops a success. Send me an email relating your experiences of these workshops.

Preparation

- Company mission/vision/strategy from Chairman's Report in Annual Report or website.
- Scope of project from project proposal and scope document.
- Objective of workshop from project sponsor or project manager.
- Personal objectives of CEO, project sponsor and project manager.
- Scope and context of workshop.
- Audience – name, role, title.

- What personal conflicts and politics in the group, and where is power?

- Terminology – what will turn them on, turn them off, no-no's.

- How much understanding and buy-in does the audience have of processes and the IOM?

- What pain has to be resolved?

- Where is ROI?

- Get Non-Disclosure Agreement signed (for external facilitators).

Agenda/sequence

- Introductions – go around the room.

- Introduce session – why they are there, pain, …

- Objectives of the session – working meeting to get a result.

- Benefits of session –
    - defines company operational strategy
    - sets context for specific projects
    - sets priorities for improvement projects
    - kick-starts projects
    - identifies project sponsors and demonstrates support.

- Show 'finished product' – so they know what they are aiming at (include showing them the attachments and measures).

- Explain benefits of the IOM if necessary.

- Strategic objectives on whiteboard (tangible – with measures).

- Mapping from end-point back.

- Identify process owners.

- Identify priority processes for initial projects
- Next steps.

Conducting mapping

- Get interaction and momentum – get them talking/arguing.
- Start with blank sheet.
- Start at back end of process 'bill and collect payment' because it is easy, non-contentious and it gets the ball rolling.
- Then map until you reach the initial step in the process.
- Don't worry about inputs and outputs initially, but as the debate grows between audience about the context and scope of each activity, use the input and output to define.
- If your software allows annotation (and it should), use it to document what the lower level activities are (if and when they get talked about) – try to avoid drilling down, as it distracts from the top level.
- To get them to focus on activities, use 'I have just joined your organisation as a Sales Manager, and I need to raise an invoice. How do I know what to do next? How do I know when I've finished?'
- If they cannot agree, move to a whiteboard to sketch a flow of processes, then go back and map them.

Issues, objections

- Can't agree on certain activities
  - revert to whiteboard
  - try to define inputs and outputs
  - look to CEO/sponsor to resolve.

- Don't have the correct people in the room
  - check if workshop results will be considered 'agreed'
  - look to CEO/sponsor to resolve.

- People focus on departments or reporting lines not processes
  - Ask the 'I do receivables, how can I understand what to do?' questions.

- IT-focused people describe in systems (automated process) terms rather than the complete process
  - Ask the 'I do procurement, how can I understand what to do?' questions
  - Put systems as resources.

Finally . . .

- WWW – What Went Well? Get points on whiteboard.

- EBI – Even Better If? Get points on white board.

- Next steps?

Summary

Chapter 26

Wrapping it all up

How do you really deliver results on all the initiatives and projects in your company? The answer is <u>adoption</u>. Through adoption everyone in your company ensures that your strategy gets implemented and that you obtain visible results from your initiative.

I put this succinctly in the formula: $R=IA^2$ (Results = Initiatives x Adoption^2).

Maximising Results by successful Adoption of the transformational changes driven out of the Initiatives. In other words, it does not matter how many initiatives (projects, exercises, and programmes, whatever) you throw at people if no one adopts the results of them. Typical initiatives include Six Sigma, software implementation (SAP, Siebel etc), Cost Reduction, Sarbanes-Oxley and outsourcing programmes.

While this may sound obvious, the corporate landscape is rife with these initiatives in progress, where little or no thought has been put into how to make sure that the rest of the organisation actually adopts and owns whatever improvement is advocated. Little surprise, then, that the adoption rate (and hence the success rate) of initiatives is pitifully low in many companies.

Gaining adoption is a challenge, not least because it involves changes in behaviour and attitudes. Inspirational leadership helps kick-start adoption throughout the company, but it cannot sustain the necessary continuous improvement required for companies to stay competitive. Adoption has measurable results, as the dramatic benefits obtained by the success stories reveal.

Adoption means communicating the changes required of people – and getting people to make the changes. The approach I am suggesting is applicable to virtually every initiative and it is achievable as it makes change as painless as possible. This is where a common language is required – an operational language which can describe the changes in activities, behaviour and results that are expected.

This language describes activities, roles and measures, and is managed through the use of an Intelligent Operations Manual (IOM). It manages processes, documents, resources and metrics – and the relationships between them. This is made possible by current IT infrastructure and software. Use of this IOM enhances accountability and serves to further adoption. And once the IOM is in place it can be applied to other initiatives and therefore increases their return on investment.

From the experience of countless client engagements my colleagues and I have identified a 5-step methodology to develop and manage the IOM. These steps build on the principles of adoption, but set them out in a practical blueprint for action.

Once you have worked through these steps, it will be remarkable how the barriers to change seem to disappear. The current business issues of compliance, the introduction of enterprise software applications and outsourcing all provide new challenges to business leaders. It is essential to get these right, and applying this new approach to these issues enables you to control and transform your business. It even keeps the strategy and your objectives to the fore when a business faces rapid growth.

Real case studies from clients around the world, in every industry, reveal the dramatic benefits and the astonishing results achieved by putting this approach into action.

Achieving results – the easy way. Turning your strategy into reality.

Index